Warheads

Warheads

CABLE NEWS
AND THE FOG OF WAR

· · · · · · · · ·

COL. KENNETH ALLARD
U.S. ARMY (RET.)

NAVAL INSTITUTE PRESS
Annapolis, Maryland

Naval Institute Press
291 Wood Road
Annapolis, MD 21402

Library of Congress Cataloging-in-Publication Data

Allard, C. Kenneth (Carl Kenneth), 1947–
    Warheads : cable news and the fog of war / Kenneth Allard.
        p. cm.
    Includes index.
    ISBN 1-59114-007-2 (alk. paper)
    1. Television broadcasting of news—United States. 2. War—Press coverage—United States. 3. Iraq War, 2003—Press coverage—United States. I. Title.

    PN4888.T4A38 2006
    070.4'4935502—dc22

                            2006016118

Contents

• • • • •

Only one is possible: This book is respectfully dedicated to the memories of those "Other People's Kids" who gave their lives for this country while serving on combat operations in Iraq. Numbering more than twenty-five hundred at this writing, they include Capt. James Funkhouser and PFC Kristian Menchaca from my adopted home state of Texas, as well as the two brave but anonymous young Americans you will meet in this book. God bless them all.

There is no greater love than to lay down one's life for one's friends.

John 15:13 (NLT)

Acknowledgments

· · · · ·

This book was a long time in the making. A string of New York publishing houses didn't get the concept of *Warheads*, and for a while it seemed doubtful that the funny stories, insider views of TV studios, and even our front-row seats at some fairly important recent events in history would ever exist as more than pleasant memories and disconnected recollections.

That this book is now in your hands is due to either the faith or the sheer wishful thinking of Tom Wilkerson, publisher of the Naval Institute Press. Tom, a former Marine major general, was an invited guest at some of our Pentagon briefing sessions and, thus, was in a privileged position to understand their importance and the story we were trying to tell. Tom and his staff, particularly Eric Mills and Inger Forland, are due our warmest thanks. Acknowledging such indebtedness to the Navy is a difficult burden for a former soldier, of course, but there are many such indignities these days.

My primary debt is to my Warhead colleagues, beginning with my pal Jed Babbin, who originally coined the phrase. That group is somehow exclusive but necessarily informal—there are no membership rosters, annual meetings, or ID cards. However, the following gentlemen were especially helpful in the writing of this book, and their contributions, like our friendships, are acknowledged here without regard to rank: Bob Scales, a genuine scholar in his own right as well as the former commandant of the Army War College, reviewed the entire manuscript and suggested a number of changes that greatly improved it. Dave Grange, Paul Vallely, Tom McInerny, Wes Clark, Don Shepperd, and Bill Cowan provided insights into their respective networks, as well as advice that proved invaluable. My NBC and MSNBC colleagues—Barry McCaffrey, Wayne Downing, Rick Francona, and Jack Jacobs—are comrades in arms and trusted friends who gave freely of their time and wisdom. Tara Jones of the Pentagon public affairs office invariably provided personable and professional assistance to my numerous requests for information. Torie Clarke, an accomplished author and a key figure behind the events in this book, was generous with her time.

The reader may sense in these pages the occasional hint of a spiritual journey, however unlikely the traveler. If you're on one of those too, then you may be lucky enough to have an entire rifle squad of friends and counselors like these: Howard R. "Biddy" Bates and Monsignor Tom McSweeney as well as Pastors Don Smith, Jim Shettler, and Max Lucado. But the same "rules of engagement" apply to these gentlemen as to the Warheads. All were kind enough to point the way: responsibility for any mistakes on these pages, and elsewhere, is entirely my own.

CKA
San Antonio, Texas
July 4, 2006

Acronyms

· · · · ·

BDU	battle dress uniform
CENTCOM	(United States) Central Command
CIA	Central Intelligence Agency
CINCs (pronounced SINKS)	formerly, commanders in chief of the U.S. combatant commands
CRS	Congressional Research Service
CSIS	Center for Strategic and International Studies
ESP	extrasensory perception
FEMA	Federal Emergency Management Agency
FUBAR	fouled up beyond all recognition (or words to that effect)
GEOINT	geospatial intelligence
GOOFI	Informal U.S. Military Academy term for "Graduates of Other Fine Institutions"
GPS	global positioning system
HUMINT	human intelligence
IED	improvised-explosive device
IFB	audio earpiece used in television studios
JAG	judge advocate general
JDAM	joint direct attack munition

KGB	Soviet Union's Committee for State Security
KLA	Kosovo Liberation Army
MREs	meals ready to eat (as distinct from meals ready to digest)
NATO	North Atlantic Treaty Organization
NCO	noncommissioned officer
NFL	National Football League
NGA	National Geospatial-Intelligence Agency
NPR	National Public Radio
OCS	Officer Candidate School
ORB	officer record brief
PDA	personal digital assistant
PGM	precision-guided munition
POW	prisoner of war
RMA	revolution in military affairs
ROTC	Reserve Officers' Training Corps
SECDEF	secretary of defense
SNAFU	situation normal: all fouled up (or words to that effect)
TPFDL	time-phased force deployment list
UAV	unmanned aerial vehicles
UN	United Nations
VFW	Veterans of Foreign Wars

Prologue

· · · · ·

Despite living in a nation at war, we Americans are as likely to know a resident of North Dakota—by population, our 48th smallest state—as a soldier serving on active duty in the United States Army. Including Reserves called to the colors, the Army's ranks contain a little less than 600,000 people, while North Dakota's human population is just over that same number. Put another way, there are roughly 1.4 million men and women serving in uniform—Army, Navy, Air Force, and Marines—with the mission of protecting all 300 million of their fellow citizens.[1] It is hardly surprising that the only soldiers we usually see are the ones we pass in the airports or glimpse on TV, where the endless supply of fresh combat videos can easily create the illusion of familiarity. Like the shadows in Plato's cave, however, those flickering images are deceptive because they convey only the half-truths of war—not the reality. And that, you see, is our problem: As a society, we are increasingly separated by the inequality of sacrifice into an electronic form of the Great Divide, with Citizen-Soldiers on one side and Armchair Warriors on the other. TV today has become what the Coliseum was to Ancient Rome, substituting a video-to-viewer reality for the first-hand experience of actually being a warrior, a disregarded heritage that as recently as the Greatest Generation was considered vital to the defense of our country. The Romans, of course, lacked remote controls, but their civilization fell when citizens became too bored, too preoccupied, or too lethargic to send their sons to defend the outposts of empire against the barbarians.

American society is not quite so decadent, or at least not yet. But have you noticed that our defenses against the new barbarians seem to be chronically short of soldiers? That the new Citizen-Soldiers we *do* have always seem to be someone else's kids? And that far too many of them seem to be drawn from the good-kids-with-limited-expectations ranks of the Red State lower-middle classes? When you want to know how they're doing in combat, you turn on the TV—our Electronic

Coliseum—and that's where you're likely to encounter the Warheads—those *other* soldiers you see on TV. We might be getting a little older, but we're still somewhat telegenic; instead of being clad in desert camouflage, however, we will more likely be wearing pinstriped suits, makeup, and IFBs—those earpieces the control room uses to tell us when to "wrap," meaning shut up pronto. The term *Warheads* was coined because we were talking heads who were on the air only because we knew about war; it gradually began to refer to the highly visible corps of military analysts that NBC, CNN, and Fox turn to whenever breaking news or developing crises demand special coverage. What all that means is this: for the last eight years or so, I have been one of those trusted experts. Along with providing expertise, I have helped to perpetuate some of those illusions of reality you have been witnessing on TV.

Why were they illusions? Because there is a vast difference between the realities and the perceptions of war as well as—forgive me for this one—between the coaches and the couches. What I mean is this: while the Warheads tried hard to be your expert coaches, your somewhat affable guides to what was happening on the battlefield, we could only be partially successful in bridging the gap between our experience as soldiers and your couches there at home in the Electronic Coliseum. That experience had inevitably separated us from the lifestyles, habits, and values of civilian culture, but we owed our presence on TV to three factors:

- Some of us were heroes but most were not. Our real credentials were that we were experts in the theory and practice of war, but, more importantly, we were also reflective enough to rise above it (even if only at a low hover).

- We were able to articulate our expertise to the audience—meaning that we were succinct and occasionally funny but had the ability to explain complex things in simple terms.

- Whatever our military rank and accomplishments, we had been able to sublimate our sometimes colossal egos to the inherent indignities of dealing with the press and the manifold inconveniences of cable TV.

All of which put us in approximately the same position you may have been in if you have ever stepped from the dock onto the deck of a small boat (the dislike of that experience was why some of us became soldiers in the first place). As we became Warheads, we somehow morphed into denizens of a demiworld suspended between two competing institutions—and we often succeeded only in spreading dismay and alarm in both places. The media, as an institution, tells all, uncovers much, and just lives for the "gotcha" of investigative journalism. The military, as an institution, is like Plato's description of the Guardians: a repository of history and tradition; a protector against the harsh realities of war, which society would prefer not to know; and, because all warfare is about deception, an instinctive manipulator and keeper of secrets. The uneasy compromise between the media and the military that created the Warheads also created the three-minute-or-hopefully-less Impressionism of our usual TV appearances. This book is an attempt to connect those dots without the limitations of those formats. So a fair warning up front is necessary: you will note in the pages that follow a fair amount of back-and-forth between analysis (what we saw or know) and opinion (what we suspect or believe). Take both for what they are worth because in this society, the perspectives of the soldier are very different from those of the civilian—which was also one of the major reasons for this book.[2]

So forget about the sound bites. This book is far more complex than anything I could ever get away with telling you about on TV and much, much tougher. Because in these pages you will learn all about the contrast between the new realities of warfare in the information age, the continuing illusions of the Electronic Coliseum, and how those discontinuities are not only a threat to our defenses but also to our democracy. Because the technologies used to prosecute the war are precisely the same as those used to report it, the resulting images are to reality what Fantasy Football is to the National Football League (NFL). Unfortunately, our political leaders prefer to believe that the electronic Great Divide is a fault line in our society best left undisturbed, even if it means compromising our defenses and substituting high-technology "solutions" rather than providing the soldiers we really need. The irony is that, even before 9-11, our enemies understood that fault line far better than we do now. Theirs is a mobilization without limits, while ours is one of uneven or nonexistent sacrifice. That's why they think they can win and why they may well be right.

Those enemies might also be crazy, but they would have to be truly obtuse to miss all the unconscious signals we send. Every two years, our fault lines are extended anew with the election to Congress of people with even less military experience than their predecessors. We have clearly forgotten all that troublesome business about the war-making responsibility of Congress—and that those making policy need firsthand military experience. Not only is this true of our current leaders but we are also guaranteeing the ignorance of the next generation. If you think I'm kidding, then consider just two revealing facts:

1. The nonpartisan Congressional Research Service (CRS) reports that the present Congress is merely the latest one to exhibit the much longer trend of

steady declines in military service; of the current bunch, just over 25 percent of the members (141/535) report such affiliations. While CRS is non-partisan, Congress is their immediate boss and writes the checks; so its analysts rather delicately point out that this figure *just might* reflect the end of the draft in 1973.[3]

2. What about preparing future leaders to prevail in the decades-long struggle with terror? At Harvard, the graduating class of 2005 (1,590 strong) produced a grand total of just *seven* seniors (0.44 percent) accepting commissions in the nation's armed services—a record which moved then-president Lawrence Summers to deliver a memorable tautology: "Our country is strong because it is free and it is free because it is strong. That would not be true without those who are prepared to commit themselves in the armed forces of our country."[4] What was tactfully left unsaid was that the vast majority of those making such commitments would presumably lack Harvard diplomas, an unintended parallel with Roman decadence that neither President Summers nor the Classics faculty would have welcomed.

As recently as the days of John F. Kennedy and Richard M. Nixon, it was an article of faith among ambitious youth that military service was virtually a prerequisite for either elective or appointive office. But by giving a free pass to the current crop of Congressional leaders, we have inadvertently sent an even stronger signal to the next generation's elite-in-training at institutions like Harvard that self-sacrifice, patriotism, and military service will not be the common virtues expected of tomorrow's uncommon leaders. Instead, the tacit acceptance of the "it's all about me" ethos from current and future leaders is not far removed from a declaration by the larger society that we had decided to reverse the evolutionary process and turn the entire herd back toward the swamps and the primeval ooze. It is a tragedy, one worthy of that poignant line from *Julius Caesar* borrowed by Edward R. Murrow for his last sign-off: "The fault, dear Brutus, lies not in our stars but in ourselves."

So blame everything on Bush, Cheney, and Rumsfeld if you want to because their record has been—as the secretary of defense himself might put it—"imperfect." But please keep in mind that they are in office solely because you placed them there—and they were confident that if anyone questioned whether America had chosen wisely, they were probably talking about the TV show, *American Idol.* Because there are some points you may have missed along the way, this book tells you how and why the following things occurred:

- How ending the draft in 1973 in favor of an all-volunteer "professional force" has created an enduring fault line on our society because when the youth were no longer compelled to serve in the military, their elders stopped caring very much about it. Now this "not in my backyard" syndrome has become the ultimate cop-out: "Send somebody else's kids to war." Failing to ensure equal sacrifice is a sure way to lose a war because it places intolerable pressures on a sociological fault line that normally lies unnoticed and undisturbed. But when those pressures build up—especially those handmaidens of war called time, taxes, and casualties—fault lines have a way of suddenly giving way and producing earthquakes and tidal waves, to say nothing of retreats.

- Although the phrase "Bowling Alone" has become synonymous with the phenomenon of American social disengagement in recent years, there are few linkages drawn between that problem and the issue of service to the nation in a time of war. Yet one of the most fateful of all symbols of social corruption is what happens when a society fails to inculcate the basic values of self-defense in its ordinary citizens, values like sacrifice, patriotism, and commitment. And the only reason we have a fighting chance in Iraq today is because the soldiers who embody those values are fighting heroically while the rest of us merely watch from our armchairs and sofas in the Electronic Coliseum.

- From Iraq to Afghanistan, much of what we think of as "the fog of war" (a term coined by the nineteenth-century Prussian strategist Carl von Clausewitz) really isn't fog at all. What you are looking at is much older: the Greeks called it "hubris." Whatever you call it, Pentagon leaders ignored an impressive amount of military history to see the war they wanted to see, rather than the nasty, violent, supremely dirty business that war really is.

- None of those civilian leaders in the Pentagon are liars, but they are true believers, which may be even worse. You see, Rumsfeld's "transformation revolution" is primarily based on the idea of substituting high technology for manpower, of curing inefficiency with a healthy dose of information-assisted rationalism. In an information age, of course, some of that makes sense; but if you're a true believer, it's difficult to grasp the idea that it might take even more of those low-technology devices called "soldiers" or "marines" to pacify a country than it did to conquer it in the first place.

- A lot of what is truly important in war involves adaptation—especially which side adjusts best to the unexpected. However, some things should not take you by surprise—and manpower is one of them, especially when it comes to the gritty reality of fighting an insurgency. Insurgencies consist of small cells conducting random attacks in which there are few effective substitutes for dusty boots on the ground. Nevertheless, Rumsfeld & Company overstretched the active force, effectively drafted the reserves, all while castigating the "red herring" of conscription.

- Sometimes, though, you have to give credit where credit is due: Under Rumsfeld, Pentagon "spin" has become an art form that reflects an extremely perceptive understanding of information-age facts of life. In both ancient and modern warfare, you try to target any element that affects the competitive environment. Nowadays that means influencing the media, wherever and however possible. If that seems a little cold, then grow up—it's a tough world out there and any public relations executive worth his or her salt would tell you the same thing. In fact, anything less and the Rumsfeld crowd would be derelict in their duties—and derelict they ain't.

- Rather than serving as a watchdog, the media—especially cable TV—has effectively become an enabler of this manipulation. Particularly in a country where personal military experience is in such short supply, normal coverage of the war amounts to momentary glimpses through a soda straw. The Warheads were long accustomed to the fundamental tensions between great issues, pop culture, and higher ratings. But particularly during the election of 2004, our perspectives were often sacrificed to the limitations of format, attention span, and competing agendas. Worse yet, we often found ourselves contributing to insane on-air discussions about the Vietnam service records of the candidates, interspersed with ratings-boosting reports from "celebrity journalists."

Troubling as those points are, the fact is that I could have written at least some of them all the way back while serving as a West Point faculty member or dean of the National War College. What makes this book unique is that it draws upon our individual and collective experiences as Warheads—as privileged, firsthand witnesses to the overlapping worlds of the military and the media. As war with

Iraq drew closer in 2003, we were getting lots of airtime—and who knew what we might say? Under the polite fiction that we were now "retired military advisers to the secretary of defense," the Warheads were soon invited to Rumsfeld's executive conference room for exclusive, off-the-record briefings—an initiative that grew into a campaign. How extensive a campaign was it? It started in 2002, continues through the present and involved seventeen closed-door meetings between the Warheads, the secretary and his key lieutenants, as well as eighty conference calls between the Warheads and top commanders, and even Pentagon-sponsored trips to the war zone. None of these contacts were either unethical or improper because we were all consenting adults and went with the full knowledge and approval of our respective networks. The Pentagon's motivation was more complex but involved an exquisite appreciation that the administration's preferred version of events was far more likely to be believed if the public heard it on TV from the very same people who had the experience, credibility, and platform to refute it.

And for a time, that's the way it worked because Rumsfeld and his minions were so smooth and so persuasive that it usually took about a day or so to decompress after one of our meetings. With our military experience and personal networks of knowledgeable sources, the Warheads might well have challenged the Pentagon party line; but because we no longer carried the responsibilities of command, we were inclined to give the benefit of the doubt to those who did. And even though we were straphangers, it really did feel good to be part of the team once more, especially when three- and four-star generals regularly told you how important you were to their war efforts. Then there were the limitations of our cable TV medium: three-minute sound bites as the rule, in-depth discussions rarely attempted, and deeper meanings usually ignored. Similar misgivings about the futility of all such rationalizations must have occurred to the First Mate of the RMS *Titanic* when he heard the cry, "Iceberg! Dead ahead!" because threats to the survival of a ship or a nation sometimes become obvious only when time is running out, when warnings have gone unheeded, when thinking has become too wishful, and when "spin" morphs into self-deception.

When the self-deception becomes pervasive enough, extraordinary events can clarify the prevailing illusions, but even then you have to pay close attention. Those who say we have enough people in uniform usually do so with soothing and seductive reasoning: that our commanders in Iraq have all the forces they have requested or that our guard and reserve forces are adequate to the tasks mapped out for them by the Pentagon. For the record, I respectfully differ on both points, but you be the judge, because in September 2005, Hurricane Katrina provided what may be our last warning—and here, too, I was privileged to have a front-row seat and not one in the Electronic Coliseum either. Recent Yankee emigrants to the Alabama Gulf Coast are rightly treated with a mixture of suspicion and condescension, but Mother Nature had thoughtfully provided me with an involuntary crash course in hurricanes, beginning with Ivan, which passed noisily overhead while devastating our neighbors just fifty miles to the east in Pensacola. That experience provided essential training for Katrina, when my roles quickly segued from survivor to relief volunteer and ultimately included a brief stint as a media "embed" with the 82nd Airborne Division in flooded New Orleans. Along the way, two vital lessons for this book were underlined with unmistakable clarity: that natural disasters were only the latest pressures stretching our military forces to the breaking point, and that this scarcity of soldiers amounted to a self-inflicted wound in a country where the voluntary instincts of its citizens run deep if customarily untapped.

If survival was the first requirement, then there was some comfort in the knowledge that Katrina was forecast to come ashore between Louisiana and Mississippi, or roughly a hundred miles to the west. But as the storm blew ashore, it was so big and so powerful that even its side lobes packed a nasty punch. From dawn to dusk, the wind howled steadily between fifty and eighty miles per hour, snapping limbs, downing trees, and with its heavy content of salt, instantly browning the lush green foliage. The highest storm surge in a century piled up surf in normally tranquil Mobile Bay and inundated "transition zones" long imagined to be high and dry. It even shifted the famous World War II battleship USS *Alabama* to a new and startling 15-degree list on its moorings. Even so, we had been lucky. The sign outside one local church spoke for many in quoting First Chronicles: "We thank Thee and praise Thy glorious name." Almost as soon as the power came back on and the streets were cleared, people set about gathering relief supplies. A local businesswoman commandeered a vacant warehouse and much of the Labor Day weekend was spent filling it to the rafters with food, clothing, diapers, and toys for the refugee families who were already flowing in from harder-hit areas.

A group from the campus church of Pensacola Christian College invited me along as they reached out to one of those areas, Pascagoula, Mississippi, a coastal community next bay over from us. What had come onshore there was not just wind and rain, but also an American tsunami that swept all before it. Senator Trent Lott's house—removed cleanly from its foundations—was only the best-known example of a devastation more thorough than most war zones; the twenty- to thirty-foot wave had left flotsam and jetsam in treetops that now overlooked acres and mountains of rubble. Yet somehow hope survived. As with Ivan, mobile kitchens from the Salvation Army and the Red Cross were everywhere, and so were SUVs, trucks, and even station wagons bearing the logos of every conceivable religious charity. Our contributions focused on making immediate repairs to private homes as well as several places of worship playing crucial roles in the relief effort. As we ripped out sodden drywall from the Sunday school rooms at the rear of one church, volunteers at the front were handing out a mountain of relief supplies to needy families. As I helped one woman load boxes of food and diapers into her car, which was now doubling as the family's temporary shelter, she suddenly began to weep. "I feel so ashamed for accepting all this. Normally we're the ones helping out the less fortunate. But now that's us."

The same weekend we were in Pascagoula, the 82nd Airborne Division received emergency deployment orders to New Orleans, with the mission of helping to restore civil authority that had been badly compromised by a trifecta of incompetence at the federal, state, and local levels. Because of my peacekeeping experience and proximity to the area, the Army quickly invited me to join the 82nd as a media embed. The division was assigned to a task force staged out of a Reserve encampment near Hattiesburg, Mississippi, where I quickly headed by SUV. The camp had received a direct hit as Katrina howled north and downed trees were everywhere—one even having penetrated the roof of the barracks where we media scum were billeted. The task force was commanded by a Cajun, Lt. Gen. Russ Honore, who was already attracting considerable press attention, both for his leadership and ability to provide good copy. That day had been no exception, according to one colleague who heard the general grousing: "Got so many a you guys roun' here now, fella can't even swing a dead cat without hittin' three reporters."

Next day I was seated next to General Honore as we shuttled into the New Orleans Superdome on an Army Blackhawk. New Orleans was familiar territory, of course, but TV pictures could never do justice to the vast watery tableau of the drowned city that now unfolded beneath us. As we flew, Honore spun an unforgettable narrative of just how devastating Katrina had been. In fact, he said, had his command been given the mission of attacking the Gulf Coast region, he would have been hard pressed to have plotted a more destructive military campaign than this hurricane. Katrina had passed over southern Florida as a minimal Category I storm before heading due west and gathering strength, "reinforcing over the warm waters" of the Gulf. Shifting to the north, she had feinted at New Orleans before obliquely assaulting the Mississippi and Alabama coasts. Building combat power while keeping the opponent off-balance is the essence of a good campaign plan, which was apparently what Mother Nature had in mind all along.

But then there was more. Once ashore, Honore added, Katrina's winds had prevented all air and ground movement for more than two hundred miles inland, effectively preventing rescuers from mounting a "counterattack." Even after the storm had passed, it had taken time for air, land, and even sea forces to rally—a point utterly lost on reporters who, he added, had a way of being "stuck on stupid." The brave ones nevertheless persisted in challenging him. Later I watched him tape a television interview with an eager but obviously inexperienced correspondent, who kept asking why the military had taken "so long" to get to New Orleans and begin organizing mass evacuations. The first few times, Honore let it pass, but then a now-familiar twinkle came into his eyes. "Look," he explained with some exasperation, "getting troops and helicopters into an area, especially one hit by a hurricane, ain't easy. It's all about logistics and logistics is all about planning. 'Cause if logistics were easy, we wouldn't call 'em logistics: we'd call 'em *tactics*."

Despite what some reporters may have thought, the 82nd Airborne Division had deployed to New Orleans only hours after receiving its first alert notice. Their commander, Maj. Gen. Bill Caldwell—a tough, rangy paratrooper—reminded me that strategic deployments were why the division existed in the first place. The Combat Infantry Badges worn by his soldiers confirmed the words, because virtually all had recently served in Iraq, Afghanistan, or both. At the first appearance of their red berets on the streets of the city, all hints of civil disturbance had instantly vanished—the only muted opposition being the baleful, resentful stares of the few New Orleans police officers who had not abandoned their posts. Still, it was eerie to be a part of infantry patrols that moved in combat formation through a dead-silent French Quarter. Residents of a black neighborhood on the city's south side filtered through an aid station the medics had set up in an abandoned high school, while division engineers in front-end loaders pushed the worst of the debris out of the streets. Some of the engineers had also cleared an area behind Saint Louis Cathedral where oak trees had fallen around a statue of Jesus. In an impromptu but moving ceremony that afternoon, General Caldwell and his Command Sergeant Major returned the statue's detached finger to Archbishop Phillip Hannon—himself a World War II veteran of the division.

Wherever you looked the military was performing hyperactive prodigies of peace-keeping. While no one had placed them in charge, they projected a quiet competence that had its own authority and they helped to align relief efforts that otherwise would have gotten in each other's way. One night, after hearing President Bush speak not five miles from where they were deployed, I watched as the brigade command staff smoothly swung into a "situation update briefing," compiling an overview of the significant events of the last twelve hours and setting overnight objectives. Action officers cryptically summarized the status of key functional areas: communications, logistics, transportation, medical, and even public affairs. Liaison officers from federal and civilian agencies participating in the recovery operation took notes as well as reporting on their own efforts. Similar briefings were taking place every twelve hours at division headquarters as well as in General Honore's joint task force. The military calls those standard procedures "battle command" and in New Orleans their application to a domestic peacekeeping mission harmonized the efforts of a host of civilian agencies simply because the military understood what had to be done and had the organizational expertise to do it.

It turned out to be one of the pockets of competence in a relief effort that became far better known for bureaucratic bungling—like Federal Emergency Management Agency (FEMA) trailers delivered without house keys or a caravan of ice that was misdirected from state to state without ever getting to where it was needed. Such fumbling occupied the attention of the nation in the weeks after Katrina, as yet another hurricane threatened western Louisiana and east Texas. The National Guard and reserve forces still performing critical functions after Katrina were moved back and forth like pawns as the new storm defied all predictions— Mother Nature's feints and misdirections again. There was also a poignant note when General Honore was there to welcome the planes bringing back home a battalion of the Louisiana Guard that had just completed their year of combat duty in Iraq, including his son, a sergeant with the unit. Now many of the returning veterans had lost jobs, homes, or both. Yet few people saw all this and drew what for me was the obvious conclusion: the active and reserve forces of the United States were being stretched to their limits, scandalously so given what was being demanded of them. And yet few national leaders were apparently willing to reach the obvious solution, get up before the cameras, look the nation in the eye, and tell it what it so desperately needed to hear: "Ladies and gentlemen, we are a nation at war and we are running out of soldiers. We need more of them and we need them as soon as we can get them in uniform. While I am not yet convinced it is the answer, we also need to examine all possible alternatives to raise those forces, including the return of the draft."

What was even more ironic was that it didn't require a particularly vivid imagination to conceive of the same announcement in considerably more stark terms, like that "iceberg dead ahead" thing. Back during the Cold War we had regularly conducted simulations and other scenarios designed to "size the force," to tell us if we had enough soldiers to fight one, two, or more wars at the same time. We always seem to reach the interesting and possibly optimistic conclusion that we had enough for two-and-a-half, assuming a decent half-war loomed somewhere. And yet now we had

- a fully developed war in Iraq, with about 130,000 troops committed;

- that elusive half-war which kept on cooking in Afghanistan;

- while it was a demanding task to tell precisely where and how many, the new "global war on terror" seemed to be keeping a lot of troops busy in new and interesting places;

- continuing commitments in places like Korea, Japan and Europe, including the newly expanded countries of the North Atlantic Treaty Organization (NATO) alliance;

- territorial defense was one of the Army's traditional missions although we always "assumed it away" in our war games; but there is now increasing evidence that control over the American border is intolerably lax for a nation professing to be concerned about future terrorist attacks.

Any idea what might happen if a few of these bills all landed at the same time? If we had, let's say, a hurricane *and* a terrorist attack on one of our major cities? And that's saying absolutely nothing about the potential for major wars with North Korea, Syria, Iran, or the nightmare thought of a coup in nuclear-armed Pakistan. Call the scenario alarmist if you want to, but remember those words the 9-11 Commission used time after time in trying to unravel why our intelligence agencies had been asleep at the switch: "a failure of imagination." So let's exercise ours just a little bit in these pages, beginning not only with bad things happening to good people but also imagining what would occur if they happened all at once. My guess is that if they did, the U.S. government would lose little time in ending our generation-long experiment with the all-volunteer force and come right after our sons and daughters. Before that happens, it's time for a little straight talk about your relationship with your military, the kind of straight talk you're increasingly unlikely to get on TV. Make no mistake, this book is not intended as a tract for draft resumption. However, in its pages you will see how we have outsourced the whole idea of national service to one's country in time of war, how we have become disengaged from a politico-military process originally meant to engage ordinary citizens, and how the Electronic Coliseum is a poor substitute for the continuing obligations of a free people. That story is told not just by me but with the assistance of my fellow Warheads, all of us frequent, if semi-invited, guests into your living rooms. Take my word for it, they're an interesting crew, and what we have to tell you now are the things we could never get away with saying on TV.

[1] Manpower statistics from the Office of the Chief of Army Public Affairs, Office of the Assistant Secretary of Defense for Manpower and Reserve Affairs and U.S. Census Bureau. Available at http://quickfacts.census.gov/qfd/states/38000.html.

[2] Although the words here are my own, many of the thoughts contained in the preceding two paragraphs are properly attributed to my friend Maj. Gen. Bob Scales, former commandant of the Army War College, currently a senior military analyst with Fox News—and the only one whom the other Warheads trusted completely to back-stop my draft.

[3] Their exact words: "This may be attributed in part to the end of the Selective Service System draft in 1973." *Membership of the 109th Congress: A Profile*, CRS Report to Congress, May 31, 2005.

[4] Quoted in the *Harvard Gazette*, June 9, 2005.

CHAPTER ONE

Soldier-Scholar

· · · · ·

Want to know how I came to be at MSNBC in the first place? The answer is that everything I have ever done on television is due to Bill Clinton. No, I really mean that: because every time the president got in trouble, it seemed like he launched cruise missiles at places most Americans couldn't find on a map. And whenever he did, Fox, CNN, or MSNBC had me on to explain the basics—where this place was; why the Serbs, Hottentots, or other groups of angry villagers now hated us; what did it all mean—and hopefully in two minutes or less. If one had a taste for ironies, they were everywhere. A generation had passed since we ended conscription—a form of crowd control and social hygiene that for much of the twentieth century introduced a constant cohort of ordinary Americans into the mysteries of life in the armed services. As a much younger man, Clinton had avoided such plebeian nastiness altogether. As president, he initially seemed intent on leading us into the sunny new uplands of international peace and cooperation where the military might be usefully altered into a kind of Sierra Club in uniform.

But peace was proving elusive as well as a complete pain in the ass, with the cruise missile taking up the slack as the all-purpose tool of diplomatic signaling. Those head-turning TV tones accompanying the somber announcement "We bring you this special NBC/CNN/Fox report" were heard more and more often, but the pervasive military illiteracy of the TV audience gave them few clues about what all the crisis coverage really meant. Even before 9-11, the cable TV business had responded with more "in-depth analysis" (which of course it wasn't) of military stories and inadvertently conjured the Warheads into existence. Brother officers known and admired from our days in uniform together now morphed into on-air interlocutors, debating partners, and fellow travelers on a media junket few of us would have imagined for a postmilitary career. The gentlemen you will meet in this book had unique military records, from four-star generals like

Wayne Downing and Barry McCaffrey to a Medal of Honor recipient like Jack Jacobs. What we had in common, though, was an ability to know—or guess—what was going on and to communicate those judgments on TV. Our audience consisted of nice folks who were good citizens and taxpayers but denizens of the Electronic Coliseum that had become the modern American substitute for military experience.

The presence of such distinguished colleagues prompts an obvious question: Why am I telling you all this? The short answer is that I am the draftee who became the soldier-scholar—a trainer, teacher, and educator whose main platform eventually became the TV studio. More importantly I experienced "up close and personal" some key parts of what used to be our common history but which these days most Americans have either forgotten or simply never learned: how we began as a nation of citizen-soldiers, became separated by the Great Divorce, and eventually segregated into a society where the soldier always seems to be somebody else's kid; and where our only contact with him or her is likely to be through the TV screen—that Electronic Coliseum which substitutes so poorly for the first-hand experience the Founders always assumed would be a continuing obligation of citizenship. When most politicians find the nerve to bring it up, their discussions of conscriptions tend to be incomplete, and when you hear a politician brave enough or dumb enough to call for a return of the draft, what you really have is someone trying to make headlines. So consider this as an overview and me as your eyewitness, because there are some essentials about our untaught common history that we need to be clear about right up front.

That history really does matter, now more so than ever, though perhaps a word of warning is in order, also up front. I am a contrarian by nature and an iconoclast by choice. At my retirement from the military, a dear friend read a passage attributed to General Grant when he was describing one of his favorite hounds: "He wasn't much to look at, and mostly did what he wanted. Lots of times that meant sleeping on the porch, where, if you spoke to him, he might cock an ear, though maybe not. But when he was on a hunt and had the scent, that dog would go and go...until whatever you were huntin' was dead."

But if you prefer an insight from more contemporary culture, you may remember that "You can't handle the truth!" courtmartial scene from the 1992 movie *A Few Good Men*. While the rest of the audience applauded the performance of Tom Cruise as the Navy JAG (Judge Advocate General) Lt. Daniel Kaffee, I clapped in all the wrong places during Jack Nicholson's amazingly accurate portrayal of Marine Col. Nathan R. Jessep. When Jessep talked about guarding freedom's wall with guns, a few good men knew from personal experience exactly what he was talking about. In the end, when Jessep lashed out that the words we used, like duty, honor, and loyalty, were an unshakable code, we understood that too. And when he concluded that those same words elsewhere were not core beliefs but simply punchlines, I was standing and cheering. But of course Hollywood wrote the ending and Nicholson was quickly dragged off to disgrace and probably incarceration by Cruise and his henchmen. But it is interesting to wonder how that ending might differ today, after everything that has happened to us since 9-11.

It had not always been that way, of course. For me the journey began in 1969 as one of the last draftees of the Vietnam era, although strictly speaking, I was a "draft-induced volunteer" who saw the handwriting on the wall and enlisted for Officer Candidate School (OCS). After commissioning me as an intelligence officer (and finally noticing I looked more German than Vietnamese) the Army assigned me to an intelligence unit in Frankfurt, where the opposition was not the Vietcong but some equally determined opponents in the KGB (Soviet Union's Committee for State Security) as well as the dedicated amateurs of the West German Baader-Meinhof terrorist gang. The realization gradually dawned that it was fun being around the people who liked being in the Army and, like many other draftees, I made the transition to "lifer." It was an even more gradual discovery that conscription—an institution deeply loathed by the '60s generation—was actually one of the traditional linchpins connecting the American people with their military forces.

Yet after 1973 the hated draft was gone, a last casualty of Vietnam, replaced by an all-volunteer force that would have to be enticed to join the ranks. The top brass had harrumphed about that, but no one seemed to pay much attention; instead, the Army obediently began the steady and sometimes arduous evolution into the professional force that most Americans would recognize a decade and more later. Looking back, journalist and military historian Rick Atkinson neatly summed up the early challenges for all of us who were directly or indirectly shaped by the Army's experiences in Southeast Asia: "They stayed the course after Vietnam, when the Army was an institution in anguish, when it was an institution beset with the anarchy of drugs, racial strife and utter indiscipline. They remained true to the profession of arms and set out to make things right."[1]

Making things right sometimes involved challenges for which we had never been prepared, like the integration of women. With a volunteer force, it was senseless to exclude 50 percent of the population from our ranks, but the changes demanded a whole new set of leadership skills that hadn't been covered in OCS or anywhere else. By the late 1970s, recruiting patterns in the new volunteer force defied all predictions, and almost overnight, the troop population of the company

I was commanding became equally divided between males and females. We scrambled to adjust and to impose some sensible limits on the highly developed pairing instincts of eighteen-year-olds. During an in-briefing, one young female soldier asked me in perfect seriousness, "Sir, I'm proud to be a soldier and glad to be here. I don't smoke, drink, or do drugs. But I really *do* like to screw. Now where in this organization can I go and do that?" You try never to show it when the troops have succeeded in getting to you, and my reply could fairly be considered somewhat curt—"Not on my turf, honey!"—but it was all I could think of at the time. Similar challenges to command must have existed on both the Love Boat and Noah's Ark, but it was still proving a lot easier to instill the basic values of the soldier in people who wanted to join our ranks in the first place.

The downside was that there was evidence of a growing gap between the American people and their military, which fewer and fewer of them had ever encountered. I first became conscious of this gap during graduate school at Harvard—partial, if delayed, revenge for having been drafted and also a frank recognition by the Army that my selection for the West Point faculty now required that I be given the best of help. My time at Harvard coincided with the Iranian hostage crisis and the Soviet invasion of Afghanistan. There were inevitably protests and demonstrations, but the biggest ones were staged only when President Carter took the first halting steps toward reinstating Selective Service registration. "Hell, no we won't go," ran the prevailing Cambridge ditty. "We won't die for Texaco."

Both the location and the event had ample historical precedents going back to our earliest days: "the very term 'standing army' remained an epithet, seared into American memory with woodcut replicas of the Boston Massacre and inscribed in the Declaration of Independence as one of George III's criminal acts against the citizens of Massachusetts."[2] But at the time, an observation by one of my Harvard classmates seemed especially compelling. Yossi Ben-Hanan was an Israeli Lieutenant Colonel and one of the heroes of the 1973 Yom Kippur War, when Israel's survival as a nation hung in the balance. "That's the big difference between Israel and the United States," Yossi observed as we watched one of the protests. "Here the Army is *you*, but in Israel, the Army is *us*."

Harvard provided a unique opportunity to consider just how Yossi's Gap had come to exist. The often-thorny relationship between the American people and their military establishment would eventually form the core of my doctoral studies, first book, and abbreviated career on Capitol Hill; but there was no way of knowing back then that I had unwittingly tapped into one of the great unresolved arguments of American life. My Harvard professors included Samuel P. Huntington, whose academic reputation stretched back to the Eisenhower administration, when he first published *The Soldier and the State*, still a classic almost fifty years later.[3] For a nation then coming to grips with the permanent conflict of the Cold War and an expanded national security establishment Huntington had unearthed some useful history.

For one thing, the traditional colonial distrust of standing armies had been ratified by victory, the expeditionary forces of the British Army—one of the world's foremost standing militaries—having been outlasted, if not always outfought. The victory also confirmed other values reflecting the structure of the new American society. "I am not acquainted with the military profession," proclaimed Virginia's George Mason.[4] Huntington cites him as being typical of the other Framers because they recognized neither a distinct "military profession nor separate military skills." Instead, George Washington became the living example of the new breed of citizen-soldier whose sacrifices had helped create the Republic, which now expected both military and political leadership to be attributes of "any man of affairs." Indeed, a principle first explored in Athens was fully embraced in Philadelphia because the Founders "believed that in a free state the citizen did not cease to be a citizen when he became a soldier but rather became a soldier because he was a citizen."[5]

With such a heritage, it was tough to imagine how Yossi's Gap might have opened, because these core beliefs were the underpinnings for key Constitutional structures, especially the all-important principle of civilian control over the military, and how it should be arranged.

> The Framers' concept of civilian control was to control the uses to which civilians might put military force....They were more afraid of military power in the hands of political officials than of political power in the hands of military officers. Unable to visualize a distinct military class, they could not fear such a class. But there was the need to fear the concentration of authority over the military in any single governmental institution. As conservatives, they wanted to divide military power, including power over the armed forces.[6]

The resulting separation of powers has become familiar ground for generations of American civics students. Federal control was divided between the president as commander-in-chief and the Congress as raiser of armies, maintainer of navies, and ultimate custodian of the war-making authority; control over nominations and appointments of commissioned officers was similarly divided between the president and the senate; and even control over the reserves ("the militia") had been split between the federal government and the governors of the several states.

Checks and balances naturally produce creative tensions, including the familiar historical rivalry between Hamiltonian federalists and Jeffersonian populists. However, Huntington also pointed out a further distinction—an ongoing contest between the amateurs and the professionals that had played subtle but important roles throughout American history. Without the existence of a separate military class, the Founders simply assumed there would be no professional soldiers. The minimal military establishment they had created would be dominated by civic-minded amateurs like themselves, competing for resources, interests, and agendas in the political process just like every other American institution; this was the model of "subjective civilian control." The contrasting pattern of "objective civilian control" was different and would only become an issue much later in American history when the increasing complexity of warfare had effectively created the professional military class the Framers had been unable to imagine. Rather than being intimately connected with society, the professional military was simply put off by itself, civilian control being maintained by setting strict limits on what they might and might not do. The overall effect is that "a highly professional officer corps stands ready to carry out the wishes of any civilian group which secures legitimate authority within the state."[7] Here, too, was a potential clue about where to look for Yossi's Gap, because the isolation of the professionals might conceivably divide "them" from "us."

Competing models of civilian control are the academic equivalents of "inside baseball"—subjects normally discussed only in closed conventions of political scientists, where a high tolerance for boredom can safely be assumed. But these models also turned out to be a useful way to follow the controversies brought about by increasing demands for greater military professionalism in the nineteenth and twentieth centuries. The pattern kept repeating itself: the more complex war became, the greater the need for more professional military institutions, and at many different levels. Systematic, rigorous training was especially needed for officers to be competent to carry out their responsibilities, prompting frequent calls to establish war colleges for both the Army and the Navy. After almost a century of increasingly industrialized conflict, for example, most European armies felt that well-organized and trained general staffs were indispensable to any modern military structure, normally headed by an all-powerful chief of the general staff.

The exception was America, where every demand for such reforms always seemed to lead to an equal and opposite reaction, spawned by the accumulated weight of more than a century of highly subjective control. The detritus normally included congressional prerogatives, entrenched interests, and what appeared to be a fair amount of Alzheimer's-induced nostalgia. How else to account for the resolute complacency even in the face of the repeated debacles of the Spanish–American

War in which interservice coordination for the campaign against Cuba was nonexistent, operational planning hardly less so, and everything entrusted to improvisation or sheer luck. The Army that eventually landed in tropical Cuba was clothed in heavy wool uniforms and forced to subsist on a diet of what was called "embalmed beef."[8] As its transports approached the shoreline, cavalry mounts were simply tossed overboard in the forlorn hope that they might instinctively swim for shore. According to Edmund Morris's account, the horses initially started swimming for Haiti, and what might easily have become the mother of all shark-feeding frenzies. Instead, disaster was averted only when a quick-thinking bugler on the beach sounded a cavalry call, causing the herd to reverse direction and paddle safely ashore.[9]

Yet in the aftermath of these near-disasters, Army reformers advocating a war college and general staff system were accused by their superiors of trying to substitute a scheme more appropriate "to the monarchies of the Old World." Their naval counterparts were similarly accused of trying to "Prussianize the Navy" and did not fully succeed in implementing a general staff within the Navy until World War II,[10] demonstrating that the struggle between the amateurs and the professionals was still alive and well. This continuing tension was all the more remarkable because increased professionalism across the military services was becoming the key to survival. In World War II, those demands reached a high-water mark, unity of command and tight teamwork between land, naval, and air forces indispensable in the integrated combat that now spanned the globe. Twelve million men and women eventually served in the armed services during the conflict, guaranteeing that formidable postwar decisions on the new defense establishment would be made in an atmosphere of unprecedented military literacy.

Partly for that reason, it took nearly three years and the direct involvement of President Truman for the National Security Act of 1947 to be hammered out—second only to the Constitution as the basic source of American civil-military relations. Creating new institutions like the Central Intelligence Agency and the National Security Council had not proven as demanding as balancing service interests in the new and supposedly unified "Department of National Defense." The new entity was a tribute to federalist principles, preserving much of service autonomy, structure, and tradition; the new "Joint Chiefs of Staff" had far less power than a typical general staff and was headed not by a chief of staff or even a commanding general but rather by a Chairman. One of the major reasons things turned out this way was the presence in Congress of many Navy veterans who were determined to protect naval aviation and the existence of the Marine Corps as a separate service.[11]

All of this seemed like a neat constitutional balance had somehow been maintained. While the Framers might have been unable to imagine a professional military class, they hadn't been able to conceive of political parties either. Yet somehow things had worked out and even flourished despite the challenges of two world wars and the long confrontation with the Soviet Union. As my graduate studies ended, it still wasn't clear where Yossi's Gap had originated: could it simply be another by-product of Vietnam-era alienation? Most of those wounds seemed to be healing, in the Army and elsewhere. But if this question was difficult to answer, it was even more difficult to remember after I checked in as a full-fledged member of the West Point faculty. The United States Military Academy is single-minded in its devotion to producing the "highly professional officer corps" that Huntington had written about—and an institution he had accurately characterized as the American Sparta. The sense of being a guest in an exclusive fraternity house was pervasive: as an OCS product, I was considered a "nongrad" or even more interestingly, a "GOOFI" ("graduates of other fine institutions").

By a happy accident my responsibilities included teaching about the 1973 legislation that had ended the draft. Only ten years later controversies that had divided the country existed only as items of historical interest, case studies for cadets who could not remember a time when military service was an obligation rather than a career choice. My draft-induced entry into the armed forces was something they found fascinating, but discussions about the antiwar sentiments of the 1960s seemed like tales from a different country, which in a sense they were. Although the College Board scores in both places were comparable, Harvard students differed from my cadets in many more ways than the "Question Authority" buttons often sported on Cambridge lapels. Harvard was assertive, insouciant, and funky, where every question might have its own moral calculus. West Point was aggressive, disciplined, and correct, where every decision reflected the deliberately inflexible precepts of the Honor Code. Those differences naturally reflected different institutional missions—Harvard being Harvard while my charges prepared for the life-or-death responsibilities of combat leadership. But it was clear that the neo-Athenian, constitutional ideal was quickly becoming an anachronism, and that the well-educated person of affairs was no longer being prepared for the smooth transition between military and political realms.

This, of course, was Yossi's Gap—the Army that had become "them" rather than "us"—but its origins seemed only indirectly related to Vietnam-era disaffection. To defuse protests against an unpopular war, the country's elites had simply ended the draft—a short-term decision that was having much longer-term consequences. However imprecise, disruptive, and occasionally arbitrary, the draft had been an important social touchstone, one of the more important bridges connecting the

American people with their military. With that bridge out, there were now no obvious ways to reconnect, and the currents of military professionalism were running faster than ever. Having won a congressional fellowship after leaving West Point, I had a front-row seat on Capitol Hill when the Pentagon command structure received its most significant overhaul since the National Security Act of 1947. The difference now was that there was little public controversy, few headlines, and even fewer members of Congress who had ever had any level of personal involvement with the armed forces they were reforming.

Nevertheless, this command structure received the ultimate test of combat just four years later in Desert Storm. Its effectiveness in that war coincided with two other overnight sensations that had previously escaped the notice of TV's elites as well as the general public: the advent of precision warfare (often accompanied by those awesome combat videos) and the noticeable improvement in the quality of the American soldier. It was unclear which innovation arrived as the greater surprise—anchors like Dan Rather heaping fulsome praises on the new breed but stopping just short of speculating on-air about where we had hidden all the dumb-asses. Actually, there weren't too many of us left by this point. Whatever its drawbacks, the all-volunteer force meant better quality straight across the board: in the capabilities of our soldiers, the embedded technology of their equipment, the more rigorous training standards that could be imposed, which ultimately meant better performance from both the soldiers and their leaders. The results had been displayed during Desert Storm in the only way that really mattered, from the Highway of Death outside Kuwait City to the famous left hook of the U.S. Seventh Corps. The latter had been the largest tank engagement since Kursk in World War II, a strategic envelopment that flanked the Iraqi Republican Guard and ended the one-hundred-hour ground campaign (the military equivalent of the ten-run rule in Little League).

All of which was why the military cared so much about professionalism in the first place, but what I had casually thought of as Yossi's Gap was rapidly widening into a chasm. One of the first people to notice was the last of a rare and dying breed, Arthur T. Hadley, a military journalist of the old school who had begun his acquaintance with the military as an enlisted tanker during World War II. After the war, he had gone on to Yale, become a print journalist for publications like *Newsweek*, and ended up covering military affairs all the way through Korea and Vietnam. In *The Straw Giant*, he coined the term "Great Divorce" to describe a military that was increasingly, if voluntarily, segregated from civil society: "[They] live in separate enclaves, they shop at company stores, they speak a company language, they attend company schools, where they study company policies alien to most of us....To a degree, this has been true of all western democracies; but in twentieth-century America this trend, this Great Divorce, has been accentu-ated."[12] The most pernicious effects of the divorce also guaranteed that "Congress and other civilian elites" would henceforth lack an effective working knowledge of the military. As a partial remedy, Hadley called for a "fair and just draft," but it was not clear how this bell should be fitted to the cat. And especially after Desert Storm no one seemed to be listening.

The public woke up again—but only briefly—after the Somalia debacle, the first military dust-up on Bill Clinton's watch. Now serving as a colonel, I was then assigned to Washington's National Defense University—a kind of in-house think tank for the Pentagon—and in 1994 was directed to conduct an official "lessons learned" study of what had gone wrong the previous year in Somalia. In a single incident in Mogadishu, the American "peacekeeping contingent" suffered one hundred casualties—including eighteen Rangers killed—in what seemed far more like war than peace. One of the least understood aspects of the post-Vietnam military was that we had become deadly serious about self-examinations and systematic improvements, but never more so than when the lives were lost and missions compromised.

My colleagues suggested numerous politically incorrect titles, but none seemed likely to clear the censors. Surprisingly, however, most of my conclusions did, because there was plenty of blame to go around. From dysfunctional international organizations—"If it looks like war, it doesn't look like the United Nations (UN)"—to convoluted commands—"If it takes longer than ten seconds to explain the command arrangements, they probably won't work"—everything about our Somalia intervention pointed to one overriding lesson that has an especially eerie ring more than a decade later: "Beware of the temptation to do too much."[13] At the UN, the White House, and the Pentagon, lots of checks were written that eventu-ally had to be cashed by the Rangers on the ground in Mogadishu. Interventions in Somalia and elsewhere may have been the cause célèbre to the politicians in New York and Washington, but there were lots of political animals in Somalia too, and the soldier ignored them at his or her peril. It may have been our intervention, but it was their turf.

There were more immediate consequences for me because writing about the Somalia experience wound up guaranteeing future invitations. Even before the report was published, my presence was being regularly requested at classified Pentagon trysts where it turned out that still more peace operations were being planned. Had this been the private sector, I would clearly have been "in" on the ground floor of either an initial public offering or a new product launch, only it wasn't. In the spring of 1996 I found myself on a different ground floor altogether—this one in Bosnia, with the U.S. 1st Armored Division. At the scene of our most ambitious peacekeeping operation to date, I was carrying the credentials of a NATO observer; that "lessons learned" thing again proving that no good deed goes unpunished.

We were our own international coalition. I started out by going on close air support exercises with the Swedes. Much as they loved peacekeeping duties, the Swedes were so deeply conflicted about their actual *military* functions that they studiously avoided any contretemps with the former warring factions. I also went on patrols with the Danes who had no such reservations: "Vyuh dida yewww-uh fire twenty-one tank rounds atta dem Serbs?" his superiors demanded of a Danish tank commander after one particularly nasty incident early in the deployment. "Because-uh eye-a did notta have-uh TWENTY-TEWWWWW," he replied to great applause each time the story was recounted in the officers' mess.

But for an old Cold Warrior it was simply mind-boggling to find myself going on combat patrols with the Russians, former adversaries who had become the next-best thing to actual allies. They knew how to fortify a position and how to site their crew-served weapons to control terrain—in short, the kind of people you could respect. One American cavalry captain summed it up best: "Sir, those guys are good. In fact, they're a lot like us. But if we had gotten into it with them, we woulda kicked their ass." Maybe so, but my more enduring memory of the Russians suggested the persistence of something more important than shared military expertise. At services one Sunday morning, the chaplain had just delivered his text—"Blessed are the peacekeepers"—before leading us in prayer. As he finished, I was startled to discover that a late arrival had slipped into the seat next to me, and that he was a senior officer from the Russian airborne brigade. It was surreal to listen again to the Sermon on the Mount while sitting next to a Soviet paratrooper. Shaking hands with him after the service, I asked how a Christian had been able to cope with life in a place where the only religion was state-sponsored atheism. His wonderfully simple answer stayed with me: "I was always *believer*."

Bosnia turned out to be an adventure as well as a sobering reminder that even the brave new world of peacekeeping looked like many other ethnic conflicts from military history. While I was in-country, the U.S. forces did not suffer even a single casualty; but the downside of success was finding that many people back home seemed to have forgotten we were there. "Oh, did you say that you were in Bosnia this summer?" one of my neighbors asked politely at a Labor Day get-together. "Didn't we hand that over to the United Nations back around Easter? Hadn't heard much about it lately," he concluded. Actually, no we hadn't, because as I was departing, the 1st Armored was preparing to transfer their responsibilities in Bosnia to another U.S. division notionally assigned to Germany, a process that was repeated for some years thereafter.

The "we–they" thing had been bad enough and maybe "out of sight" really *was* "out of mind," but it seemed like the armed forces were becoming a new class of nonpersons. Just before leaving active duty in late 1997, I came across the work of another Harvard thinker, Robert Putnam, the new dean of the Kennedy School of Government. For more than twenty years, Putnam had been studying the process of civic disengagement in the United States—the tendency for Americans to withdraw from the social institutions which had once brought them together. His research indicated that the nation's "social capital"—renewed from generation to generation in places like schools, churches, unions, and even bowling leagues— was no longer being replaced. Instead, Americans were withdrawing into water-tight compartments; instead of associations enriched by those highly socialized recreational leagues, they were now "Bowling Alone." Putnam's book became a best-seller, but as I riffled through its pages, something seemed to be missing. Beyond vague references to fading generational memories of World War II, military service was barely even mentioned. Conscription was not listed in the index, though "consensus" and "consciousness-raising groups" were; ditto the draft, losing in the cut to "downsizing" and "drugs, illegal." No matter how comprehensive, any research must necessarily exclude some things to focus on others. But it was startling how, in a work exhaustively devoted to examining the causes of social disintegration, military service, one of our greatest historic engines of social cohesion and shared commitment, had been scratched.[14]

Contemplating the end of active duty, I had given some thought on how to prepare for a second career, the preferred term to "retirement," which no matter how we try to disguise it, is a kind of public death. Where you used to meet with the personnel officer to review your officer record brief (ORB), you were now dismayed to learn that ORB stood for "Old Retired Bastard." But even before the retirement papers were final, my carefully cultivated reputation as a maverick began to catch up. Even before Somalia and Bosnia, I had been involved in one controversial issue after another: defense organization reform, procurement streamlining, and now this nasty peacekeeping business. It slowly became apparent that it was one thing to be an "outside-the-box thinker" when in uniform, but that in civilian life, the comparable term was "smartass." In the competition for government contracts, no Beltway bandit in his right mind was looking for even a single discordant note that might stampede the herd on its way to the feed lot. Among defense contractors there were sometimes even greater pressures for conformity—or "responsiveness to the needs of our government customers," as one glossy brochure proudly put it—than in the Pentagon itself.

Things were looking grim, but then an odd thing happened. Even before leaving active duty I had appeared on several PBS documentaries focusing on military affairs. Now a PBS producer phoned with the startling news that an independent production unit was putting together a documentary on the Somalia operation; they had heard I had written a book some years before on the topic, would I be interested in working with them? The money turned out to be modest but the project was first rate. Airing in the fall of 1998, *Ambush in Mogadishu* became an instant PBS classic, eventually winning an award for documentary excellence. What made the production so successful was that years before the appearance of *Blackhawk Down* as a feature-length film, it provided a firsthand account of the heroism of the Army Rangers, several of whom spoke movingly for the first time about their combat experiences. Both in the documentary and on the PBS Web site, it was deeply satisfying to go public at last, and to highlight the stark contrast between the heroism and self-sacrifice of the Rangers with the stunning strategic naïveté of those who had sent them.[15]

Meanwhile the media was providing a steady stream of opportunities for such ruminations because American foreign policy was becoming a continuous adventure. Unchallenged genocide in Rwanda proved that the enthusiasm for new peacekeeping commitments was now under firmer control. The Balkan pot, of course, still simmered, the failure of NATO leaders to bring leading Serbian war criminals to justice inevitably being read as weakness that would eventually bring forth its own challenges. But even against this troubled backdrop, Iraq was in a class by itself as the near-constant provocation for American military action. The cease-fire accords that ended the first Gulf War had led to a series of cat-and-mouse games: between the Iraqi intelligence services and the UN inspectors looking for the elusive weapons of mass destruction and between Iraqi air defense gunners and coalition pilots flying combat patrols over the "no-fly zones" that covered over half the country's air space.

One of the places that did a commendable job of covering the ensuing controversies was National Public Radio (NPR). With its relaxed format and generous time allowances, radio would become one of my regular outlets, but NPR has always had a well-deserved reputation as the left coast of American journalism. Arriving at their Washington studios for the first time, I noticed that beards and earth shoes were everywhere—and these were only the women. A staffer led me to the sound booth and introduced the moderator and fellow guests. More beards and earth shoes now complemented a nice selection of fleece pullovers: it was starting to look like a sketch from *Saturday Night Live*. Once the show started, the real worth of NPR came across because we had an entire hour for an in-depth discussion of the topic, varied points of view, and even call-ins from an astoundingly large and diverse audience.

The first call was from "Ralph of Racine, Wisconsin." Ralph's point was basically that the United States was *so totally complicit* in most of what was wrong in Iraq and the Middle East in general. Oh yeah, and the rest of the world too. Noticing that my facial muscles had begun to twitch, the moderator frowned slightly and softly intoned, "Colonel Allard?" After thanking him and NPR for the privilege of being on-air, I noted that my twenty-eight-year military career had been devoted to the defense of Ralph's right to say such incredibly stupid things before a nation-wide radio audience, that if he kept on listening he just might learn something, but that the odds were strongly against it. Well. NPR was nice enough to invite me back on a time or two after that, but not often enough to justify investing in my own earth shoes. However, I subsequently heard from friends lost since junior high school who claimed they never missed a single day of NPR. They agreed with Ralph, of course, but made it a point to thank me for my service to our country.

Our bittersweet reunion was a useful reminder of the principal point this chapter has tried to make: that service to the nation, one of the common obligations of American citizenship and celebrated as recently as the Greatest Generation, had been irretrievably lost just a single generation later. And that as a result, common bonds had been lost as well, leaving us as stepchildren of the Great Divorce, distant relations in an extended but broken family. Thinking of my schoolmates that way also made it possible to gain a different perspective because I had gotten sucked into the "them versus us" mentality as well, despite having started all those years ago as a humble, "draft-induced volunteer." For a moment I even regretted having snapped at Ralph, but only for a moment because the arrogant little prick probably had it coming. Nevertheless, the lesson was especially useful for the soldier-scholar who was about to become a Warhead, because being a color commentator in the Electronic Coliseum meant that the old (though still telegenic) professionals must put matters plainly for all the amateurs, those distant relatives who had never served a day in their lives.

---

[1] Rick Atkinson, remarks to the USMA Class of 1991, West Point, NY. Reprinted in *Prologue, Conduct of the Persian Gulf Conflict: Interim Report to the Congress*, July 1991.

[2] Joseph J. Ellis, *His Excellency* (New York: Vintage Books, 2005), 138.

[3] Samuel P. Huntington, *The Soldier and the State* (Cambridge: Harvard University Press, 1981). (Hereafter, listed as *Soldier*). Huntington later became much better known for his best-seller, *The Clash of Civilizations and the Re-Making of World Order* (New York: Simon & Schuster, 1996).

[4] Huntington, *Soldier*, 164.

[5] Ibid.

[6] Huntington, *Soldier*, 168.

[7] Huntington, *Soldier*, 84. See also my discussion of these models in *Command, Control, and the Common Defense*, rev. ed. (Washington, DC: National Defense University Press, 1996), 22–23. For a superb and succinct discussion of these issues, see Eliot Cohen's, "The Theory of Civilian Control," Appendix in his book, *Supreme Command: Soldiers, Statesmen and Leadership in Wartime* (New York: Free Press, 2002), 225–248.

[8] A good account of these difficulties is contained in Russell F. Weigley, *History of the United States Army* (New York: Macmillan, 1967), 295–312.

[9] Edmund Morris, *The Rise of Theodore Roosevelt*, (New York: Modern Library Edition, 2001), 666–67.

[10] Senate testimony of Gen. Nelson A. Miles, quoted in Kenneth Allard, *Command, Control, and the Common Defense*, 79–80. "Prussianize the Navy" was the usual epithet used by opponents of Navy reform.

[11] For a short discussion of these controversies, see Allard, op. cit., 113–24. The definitive treatments are by Demetrios Caraley, *The Politics of Military Unification* (New York: Columbia University Press, 1966) and Vince Davis, *The Admiral's Lobby* (Chapel Hill: University of North Carolina Press, 1966).

[12] Arthur T. Hadley, *The Straw Giant* (New York: Random House, 1986), 274.

[13] Kenneth Allard, *Somalia Operations: Lesson Learned* (Washington, DC: NDU Press, 1994), 89–93.

[14] Robert D. Putnam, *Bowling Alone: The Collapse and Revival of American Community* (New York: Simon & Schuster, 2000).

[15] At http://www.pbs.org/wgbh/pages/frontline/shows/ambush/interviews/allard.html

CHAPTER TWO

First Media Encounters

· · · · ·

Most human activity improves with repetition, and each media opportunity seemed to spawn others that now included occasional appearances on cable and network television. This was useful practice in learning how to connect with national audiences, but it wasn't paying the bills. Most of the networks, including a number of radio stations around the country, seemed to assume that the time and effort that went into those appearances resulted from love rather than anything as pedestrian as money. So when my friend Dan Goure called with a suggestion, there was every incentive to listen. Dan regularly augmented his think tank salary by moonlighting for a number of media outlets, including MSNBC. Now he wondered if I might be interested in devoting a whole weekend to the network's in-studio coverage at its headquarters in Secaucus, New Jersey. "And by the way, they will cover your expenses and pay you for your time." Deal! MSNBC confirmed the arrangements, and sometime later I found myself heading to New Jersey on my first gig as a paid media slut.

The route was precisely the same one that later become familiar to millions of viewers as Tony Soprano began each week's show by driving his Cadillac through the Lincoln Tunnel and into the "near abroad" of the gritty industrial communities along the New Jersey Turnpike. Urban legend has it that Secaucus once consisted mostly of pig farms, although some parts resemble the scene from an earlier gangster era, as in *Godfather I* when Clemenza executed a mob hit at the edge of a swamp just across the river from New York City and delivered the classic line, "Leave da gun. Bring da cannolis." Today Secaucus is home to a profusion of outlet malls, restaurants where Joey Zaza and Tony Walnuts would not be out of place, mom-and-pop stores that proudly display pictures of relatives serving in local police and fire departments, and acres of electronics plants and storage complexes. In the mid-'90s, one of those warehouses was gutted to the walls, sound stages were constructed, banks of monitors installed, many miles of wiring and cables connected...and MSNBC was born.

You almost have a physical shock when seeing something in person that you previously have only encountered in pictures, on TV, or in the movies. As reality replaces image, the brain unconsciously fills in the blanks that have been missing: "Look how small this place is! It seemed a lot bigger on TV!" Not so with MSNBC. When I walked in that first morning, there was a disposable camera in my briefcase for taking the pictures that would probably be my only souvenir of a one-time experience; but only a wide-angle lens could possibly have captured the sound stages and studios spread over the better part of a city block. Every TV studio I had been in until then had been a one- or two-room affair; here the central sound stage was a two-story set big enough to toss a football. The cavern contained balconies, rotating banks of overhead cameras, automatic lighting from every conceivable direction, electronic ticker tapes, clocks and monitors in the ceiling, and a computer-controlled central anchor desk that moved as the entire set shifted directions between segments. The room was even big enough to comfortably house its own news complex of producers, writers, and directors who sat within camera range as if it were the most natural thing in the world.

The rest of the complex was large enough to contain production facilities for each show, administrative offices for the whole network, video production and archives, graphics, makeup suites, and a cafeteria known as the MSNBC.COMmissary. As impressive as it all was, what made the whole place work was its ability to process the undigested data of raw news, beginning with the direct video feeds filtering in 24/7 from hundreds of satellite sources across the globe. Edited at astonishing speeds in the Secaucus control rooms by twenty-somethings ("clickers"), these video feeds made it possible for the network to transmit live pictures either of breaking news or correspondents' reports from any location in the world where it was possible to arrange portable power and a satellite uplink.

But there were other data streams as well: each computer terminal had feeds from the major wire services as well as access to the network's own internal "hot wires" file that linked breaking stories to NBC's stable of reporters, correspondents, anchors, and producers. There was finally the Internet, which had already become a new kind of news medium in its own right—uncontrolled, often misleading, sometimes flat-out wrong, but a constantly democratizing influence lest networks harden into hierarchies. As an intelligence officer, I found obvious similarities with my former profession, especially the ability to gain insights from "cross-cueing," that is, comparing multiple sources of information on the same problem. But in the Pentagon we often took days, hours, or weeks to filter information through the system in response to a commander's inquiry or even to a congressional "request for information." Here the pressure was more intense, and any delays measured in seconds and minutes.

While working as an occasional bit-player around the studios of the three major cable networks, I never had anyone sit down and systematically explain to me how any of these technologies worked or how they related to the "guest." Nor had there been any need to do so: I was in the studio only for the minimal time needed. After being constantly watched over and escorted on-camera, I was politely led out afterward. But MSNBC was different; I would be doing multiple "hits"—or on-air appearances—and between them left free to roam around. There was an obvious need to understand how things worked, if for no other reason than to avoid walking in front of a live camera at the wrong moment. (Given the broad expanse of the sound stage, this was not an unrealistic possibility.) I would be doing live appearances with an anchor, who would set me up with a question—or "toss"—which I should do my best to answer before tossing back. The answers needed to be kept short and to the point; if they ran a little long, I could expect to hear the word "wrap" in my ear, which was an unsubtle cue to shut up.

To hear those cues and other directions from the control room, I was fitted by the "hookers" in the sound crew with battery-operated kidney packs wired to an IFB and a small, lapel-mounted microphone. As these connections were being completed, I observed to Allan Neugent, the sergeant major of the stage crew, that it now seemed strange to be in a place where hookers, bookers, and clickers had such vital functions. He never batted an eye, but responded with the two best pieces of advice anyone ever gave me that weekend or in nine subsequent years with the network: "Just remember to shut your mike off before you go to the men's room. And those MSNBC coffee mugs are stage props; if you try to swipe one of 'em, I'll come and find you."

One of the anchors working that weekend was Soledad O'Brien, a rising star at MSNBC and the host of *Morning Blend*, a laid-back morning show enjoying excellent ratings. A Harvard graduate, Soledad was bright, friendly, and already had the easy mannerisms that would later make her a star at NBC and CNN. Mostly because of her, our tosses went cleanly as we discussed the latest tensions between Iraq and the United States. As morning segued into afternoon, another attractive lady, Nanette Hansen, took the chair. When one of our segments ran long, Nanette was sympathetic, pointing out that sometimes the control room forgot to give the "wrap" command, or that it was often difficult to hear in the midst of a normal conversation. "Tell you what," she added helpfully, "if you run long next time, I'll just wink at you as a signal to stop." I reacted as any normal, middle-aged male might: "Well, that *would* do it. I'm just not sure what to do about the sweating and the stammering." She was kind enough to laugh and the rest of our segments together were smoother, but there was no mistaking that being professional on TV meant being succinct.

Brief or otherwise, with some other MSNBC segments, there wasn't a lot for me to contribute. Later that Saturday afternoon, a team from one of the beauty magazines came in with a software program that analyzed facial features. In one of that weekend's highest-rated segments, it turned out that another of our anchor ladies had perfect facial symmetry, but you could already see why *Saturday Night Live* had done a hilarious sketch comparing MSNBC to a co-ed slumber party. When I returned to the studio the next morning, it seemed possible to relax a little. Clearly there were some new challenges to be met and new skills to be mastered, but there was room for some optimism as well. Sure enough, that morning's segments with Soledad and Nanette—by now old friends—went without incident. By afternoon I had settled in comfortably to the new routine, even taking time for a leisurely reading of the *New York Times* and not paying an extreme amount of attention to what was going on in the studio.

It would have been better to have recalled more about the lessons of combat, especially that rule of thumb about time being divided between 95 percent boredom and 5 percent stark terror. There was no warning, but suddenly the sound crew was at my side turning the microphone back on, makeup ladies were taking hefty whacks at me with powder puffs, and the stage manager was propelling me into the seat at the desk just opposite our afternoon anchor, Jodi Applegate. There was just time enough to hear Jodi finish reading from a news wire about the latest wrinkle from Iraq: UN Secretary General Kofi Annan had made yet another of his periodic Neville Chamberlain-style pilgrimages to Baghdad to present Saddam with the very latest and quite possibly his last and best opportunity to comply with all outstanding UN resolutions. As he had so many times before, Saddam had once again agreed, probably forestalling the latest confrontation with the Clinton White House. As the cameras swung around at me, I heard Jodi say, "Now here to discuss these latest developments is our MSNBC military analyst, Colonel Ken Allard. Well, Ken, what are your thoughts on this situation?"

This game was admittedly a little new to me, but already I could sense that the only two responses that came immediately to mind—"I have none" or "Hey, lady, beats the hell out of me"—were probably not especially helpful or appropriate. I hadn't seen the agreement or even the damned news wire long enough to form any judgment, coherent or otherwise. From somewhere deep inside, a hidden reserve of self-preservation left over from my military training took over and the "waffle gene" at last kicked in, big time.

"Well, Jodi, it really isn't clear what Saddam has agreed to, or how far it goes toward satisfying the requirements the UN has laid down. What is probably needed here is time enough to examine the agreement in detail, and then to compare it to those UN resolutions. Something like that could keep a team of international lawyers busy for a long time."

All true enough, but I sounded as if my day job was with the law firm of Dull & Boring, PC. Worse yet, during the waffling, Jodi's eyes had glazed over; I had lost her and probably the audience back home as well. The reaction elsewhere inside the studio was harder to judge. The stage and sound crews were still watching Jerry Springer reruns and paying no attention to us; but they always did that, so there was no telling. It seemed safer to shift gears on the assumption that there was probably not much else to lose.

"Look, forget about the international lawyers. Think of this agreement like you would a used car. Looks good on the lot. Maybe even feels good on the test drive. And the Blue Book value is about where it oughta be. But you know what? Until you're looking at a signed contract, with warranties and above all a payment schedule, well, you don't have anything except the word of that used car salesman."

Suddenly we had ignition, liftoff and the shuttle had just cleared the tower. Jodi was now back there in the studio with me, and just in the nick of time too. Because I now discovered something else about breaking news: it came fast and furious, it involved all kinds of players, and whoever was in the anchor chair was like a traffic cop at a particularly busy intersection. My used car metaphor had certainly been simplistic, but this wasn't rocket science and the need to define that situation—clearly and quickly—was essential. Over the next hour, Jodi smoothly handled a parade of diplomats, correspondents, analysts, government spokespersons, members of Congress, and a host of lesser prevaricators. Best of all, she was nice enough later on to thank me, and tactful enough not to congratulate me for recovering my own fumble.

Defining a situation was one of the more important things a professional intelligence officer was occasionally called upon to do, although seldom under the time constraints and other pressures of the TV cameras. But there was simply no way of knowing back then that the landscape of war into which we were heading would eventually extend from Kosovo to the close-at-hand horrors of 9-11 to the remotest corners of Afghanistan, and from a rapid, hi-tech blitzkrieg of Iraq to a protracted slow dance on its killing grounds. Along the way, the Warheads were conjured into existence, but we also made it up as we went along, a trial-and-error process of figuring out how best to communicate those new realities of war to a public largely unacquainted with the skills and perspectives of the warrior. To reach them, you first had to deal with anchors who might not know much more than their audiences. On my library bookshelf, for example, there is a much-treasured coffee cup, a memento of the last *Geraldo Rivera Live* show done on CNBC and the only time I was actually in-studio together with Geraldo. Over the preceding three years, we had done enough remote "hits" together to become quite comfortable with each other's mannerisms and expressions, but that cozy relationship was not something that you might have predicted from our first on-air encounter.

By the spring of 1999, we were at war in Kosovo—or more accurately with the Serb rump state of the former Yugoslavia—which was busy doing things to the Kosovar population that would have embarrassed the Waffen SS. Long lines of refugees pushed out of Kosovo by Serb ethnic cleansing produced televised scenes that looked like videotapes caught in a time warp from World War II. Ratings jumped and MSNBC responded by signing a retainer agreement with me, reckoning that my recent experience as a peacekeeper in nearby Bosnia meant that they could draw upon me for some reasonably well-informed commentary. A retainer was a welcome change from the usual consulting-for-table-scraps arrangement, but the understanding was that other members of the NBC family of companies were free to call on me as well, at no additional charge.

The phone rang one afternoon shortly after the retainer had taken effect. A booker for CNBC was on the line to ask if I could do an interview that very evening with Geraldo, who had just returned from Kosovo and wanted to show off some interesting new videotape. Sure, why not, and I soon found myself in the CNBC studios perched in an office building opposite one of the lesser slopes of Capitol Hill. Once there, I ran into an old friend, retired Air Force Lt. Gen. Tom McInerny, also booked as a guest on Geraldo's show. As we brought each other up to date, Tom mentioned that he had just become the new president of Business Executives for National Security. This was interesting; secretly I allowed myself the fantasy that Tom might introduce me to his wealthy new friends, and that one of those business execs might be looking for someone who was willing to shill for food (by now one of my other sidelines).

Presently we moved from the green room (which is always a green room from network to network, but never, ever green) into the makeup room (which not only had makeup but, better yet, makeup *hunnies*). Led by Patty McLaughlin, den mother of the NBC Capitol Hill studios, these ladies were and are true artisans of their craft. They were also far better looking than the usual suspects they escorted to the studios—after one last hopeful swipe of face powder. Show me a straight middle-aged male who doesn't enjoy their attention and I'll show you a liar. It is said that Washington gives ugly people a chance for the notoriety instinctively denied them by Hollywood. The makeup ladies believe in this precept absolutely and do their professional best to add to the studio guests whatever gifts nature may have denied them. Does it help? An old friend from the war college saw one of my first network hits, complimented the cogency of the yadda-yadda, and then blurted out, "You really looked good on TV, too. In fact, a lot better than you do in person." Thanks to Patty and her ladies, he was undoubtedly correct.

With our worst flaws now artfully camouflaged, Tom and I were seated side by side at a studio desk opposite several cameras. Geraldo and another guest were in CNBC's main studio, at that time located in exotic Fort Lee, New Jersey, within literal and figurative spitting distance from the George Washington Bridge. Through our earpieces we were warned by the producer that Geraldo would introduce each of us in turn and then "roll tape." He also cautioned us that while the tape was running, they would be running a "screen-in-screen" shot, that is, a small cutout of us, so that the television audience could not only view the footage but simultaneously see our reactions to it.

An interesting wrinkle about which nothing had been said up until that very moment. But that was often the way of TV producers, whose advance planning often seemed to resemble a class of eight-year-olds with especially severe cases of attention deficit disorder. "Wonder if the tape is going to be really gory?" Tom whispered. "We can only hope," I replied. It was to be one of my few coherent comments that evening. Geraldo came on, "teased" the tape he was about to show, and briefly introduced each of his guests. As the red lights shone sequentially on each of our cameras, Tom and I put on our game faces, nodded back to Geraldo, and waited to see what was coming next. It was the first time I had really watched Geraldo perform in a medium that now involved me. Despite my earlier reservations, the man was flat-out impressive in his setups and transitions. So too was his voice, with a bourbon-smooth, radio clarity that invited the audience to accompany him behind Serb lines into the breakaway province of Kosovo.

The tape began to roll and we saw a typically dense Balkan forest. Now and then we caught glimpses of the Kosovo Liberation Army (KLA) guerrillas who had smuggled Geraldo into Kosovo in much the same way they also smuggled in hashish, weapons, and any other cash crop. Although Tito's Yugoslavia had been nominally communist, the reality was always far more bohemian. Either way, these people represented a triumph of true Gordon Gecko capitalism because they would do anything if the price was right. Which was probably how Geraldo had gotten in there with them in the first place. "Wonder if those KLA bozos had enough sense to get their money up front?" Tom whispered out of the corner of his mouth. I made no reply. Even though we were retired, you couldn't very well shush a general; we were also on-air and if not at that instant on a live mike, then still fully wired for sound. Plus something else was about to happen. The rising pitch of Geraldo's ever-expressive voice was keying the audience that high drama was afoot. Sure enough, the camera showed the edge of a tree line and, amidst much rustling and whispering, Geraldo announced they were close to a Serb position. An instant later, his head and shoulders could be seen popping clear out of the bushes, presenting the kind of wide-eyed target the trophy buck always presents on the deer-shooting shows just before the fatal shot rings out.

"Why not just wave at 'em?" Tom murmured again. Again I made no reply because the only thought going through my head was that had I been along with Geraldo on that KLA patrol, I would have shot him myself. The use of cover in enemy territory is one of the first survival lessons we teach during basic combat training, the idea being that if you break cover the way Geraldo had, there is an excellent chance of attracting the attention of well-armed people who will be seriously pissed off by your very presence. If the enemy is at all competent, such an error can be fatal; but Geraldo had obviously made it back in one piece. Were the Serbs asleep? As if in answer to my unspoken question, the hand holding the camera on Geraldo visibly shook, and an instant later came the unmistakable *harrumph* and black-gray bursts of incoming artillery. Apparently the Serbs were wide awake and in no mood whatever to ask politely if anyone had a press pass. This was rapidly becoming a farce: an increasingly hilarious contrast between Upper West Side media elitism and low-rent but quick-on-the-trigger Serbs whose entire history was an eight-hundred-year grudge match. You could sense who was going to win this one, but alarmingly, the longer the tape went on, the funnier it seemed.

I now started to giggle softly but managed to keep a straight face. The tape rolled on. More shell bursts. Now I was developing what in OCS had been termed a "smile problem." Worse yet, the giggles were becoming harder to control, and Tom was becoming alarmed while trying to stifle himself as well. "Sssssssssssshh-hhhhhhhhhhhhh," he whispered urgently. It was like trying not to laugh in church—and there, too, my record was one of abject failure dating back to puberty. A group of us young hellions had always seated ourselves in the back "sinners' pews," which was fine with our parents as long as we behaved ourselves. But on an otherwise dull Sunday morning one of us—the preacher's son, no less—had gloriously and thunderously broken wind; no amount of shushing and hushing could keep me from laughing to the point of tears and beyond. Since this was a Baptist church, tears were OK, but not if you shed them in quite this way. Who knew? It might even lead to dancing!

I had been grounded for a week over that one and now tried to recall the stern lectures, even while biting my lip, tongue, and cheek in a doomed effort at self-control. I almost managed it and probably would have if that damned tape had been ten seconds shorter. But the scene shifted for the last time and now you could see Geraldo in jeans and sweater with videocam held high, sprinting head-long for all he was worth. While two more Serb shell bursts went off behind him in the middle distance, as if to hurry him on his way. It was just too much: "AHH-HHHHH HAAAAAAA HAAAAAAAAAAA HAAAAAAAAAAAA," I roared, shaking, pounding the desk and now abandoning any pretense of self-control.

The tape ended and Geraldo was on me in a flash. You could almost hear his bushy eyebrows going up and down. "Well, Colonel. I see you found our little adventure in Kosovo...*kind of humorous*?" There had been more than a few occasions in the Army when I had been chewed out by experts who really enjoyed their work: counterattacking was always the best response. And whatever else he might do, Geraldo couldn't prefer court-martial charges. Wiping my eyes, I replied, "Well actually, yes I did, while wondering how in the hell you even survived. And here is what I've come up with. The Serbs were probably given only eight artillery rounds that day—and they had already fired six of them at you. That means they decided to save the other two for a better target at the end of the day. 'Cause if they hadn't, you probably wouldn't be right here now." One of his saving graces is that Geraldo has a well-developed sense of humor and he seemed to appreciate the irony. Tom quickly joined in my rescue as well, like when the other matadors gather around to distract the bull when one of their own has been gored.

But that evening's enlightenment had been straight out of a Gary Larson cartoon. Or if your taste runs to the historical, it was a lot like when the Washington crowd went out to Bull Run one summer day in 1861 to catch a gratuitous glimpse of battle, ran straight into a fellow called Stonewall, and ran back home again even faster than Geraldo on that stretch of road. Wisely enough, Tom to date has never introduced me to any of his friends in the business executives group, but has remained a valued friend in his own right. He is also the most senior member of our merry band of military analysts, having switched channels to join Fox News, where he has become a mainstay of their coverage. It's fun to remind him occasionally that Geraldo subsequently made that same switch over to Fox, so Tom is now responsible for telling him when ducking enemy fire makes the most sense (most of the time, especially if you're anywhere close to being in range).

Before Geraldo changed networks, we had lots of other opportunities to mix it up together, and on a wide variety of issues: Vietnam anniversaries (when Geraldo actually started the show by singing the Crosby, Stills, and Nash ballad *O-HI-O*);

endless discussions over the demilitarization of the Puerto Rican island of Vieques; and more discussions on Iraq policy and operations than either of us can probably recall. After that first time, the ice had been broken, so our discussions were some of the most straightforward and fast-paced that I had with any anchor, like a good tennis match when the partners are well chosen. We have both moved on since those days, but I still miss our encounters at CNBC. My fervent hope, though, is that Fox sends Geraldo into a combat zone only when there are professionally competent military analysts close at hand.

CHAPTER THREE

The Rules of Engagement

• • • • •

Standing guidance during my teaching days at West Point and Georgetown was that the best student papers usually followed a start-to-finish story line because a simple chronology is easier for both the reader and the writer. That advice is still good, and I depart from it here with some reluctance. But perhaps you have already noticed that with the progression of hits, gigs, and other TV appearances, the Warheads had stumbled into a kind of parallel universe that TV viewers may suspect but do not themselves experience unless major portions of their lives have been wasted waving signs outside the windows of the *Today Show*. In this odd new world, things were not always what they seemed. Gradually, though, certain underlying realities became clear, often after screwups, mistakes, and the best efforts of talented people dealing with the inescapable limitations of human institutions. For all its pretensions, cable TV is a very human institution indeed; so what follows in this chapter are not chronological events but some affectionate observations of the parallel media universe compiled over nine years. They certainly reflect the limitations of the observer—this may be unique to MSNBC and uncharacteristic of CNN or Fox, where the pressures probably include the scheduling of all those Mensa meetings. So you decide.

The camera is always running, the air factory always open, and always assume that the microphone is "hot"

Some people say that all you really need to know about NBC News is that it's a branch of the NBC Entertainment division, but this structural reality is true elsewhere in the media conglomerate as well, because today all networks are parts of an infotainment service industry in which "product" has to be put out 24/7 regardless of content. Inevitably, there are more hours in the day than real news to report, or even semi-interesting facts. The immediate results are endless repetition and the ever-widening search for items to fill the void. The penetrating power of the microscope is sacrificed to yield a progressively wider field of view to the point that the distinction between local and national news is often blurred or lost entirely.

Highway accidents—if they are spectacular enough—and raging fires—if they are bright and bad enough—can tempt any producer to cut into the weightiest discussions with "this breaking news." Of course it really *isn't* breaking news or even current events. However, it is eye candy for which we have an insatiable sweet tooth, and with many, many hours to fill each day, the heavy stuff can always get shifted until later. The phrase is known as "floating," which means that program priorities have been shifted by the producer—typically a twenty-something, often sleep-deprived, and with senses overdosed to the point of insanity by the flickering, disco-like electronic images of the darkened control room. Into this cacophony he or she must induce order: so Ken's two-minute segment on the history of the Arab-Israeli conflict, the road map to peace and the future direction of U.S. strategy in the Middle East (I am *not* making this up) is now "floating" until the eleven o'clock segment because *now* we need to bring you a *spectacular* truck fire occurring even as we speak on the New Jersey Turnpike. Flames, wreckage, and propinquity—a guaranteed trifecta in any cable TV newsroom.

There is a certain amount of adrenaline that gets pumped prior to any TV appearance, and floating inevitably feels like a postponed athletic match. And no matter how experienced a veteran of the "news biz" you may be, when the word reaches you that you're floating, you are well advised to recall the most basic precept of that business: that the mike is always hot, even—and especially—if you think it isn't. We take routine and savage delight when politicians forget this basic truth, when their inadvertent racial slurs, ethnic jokes, sexual come-ons, or obscenity-laced put-downs are transmitted beyond the spin control of any apologist directly to the waiting ears of an eager audience. Those well-known facts of the politico-media world resonated strongly the first time Tim, C.J., or one of the other sound guys up at MSNBC took great care to ensure that the mike was turned on before I went on the set and even greater care that it was turned off afterward. Legends abounded of anchors rushing offstage for a pee break between segments and transmitting various bathroom indignities to riotous applause from the sound crew and the control room. There were even rumors of bootleg tapes that some said gave a whole new meaning to floating.

Now with all that history you would think that I might have been just a tad smarter about the whole business of open mikes. I was mostly, but it only takes once. My "once" came on an otherwise uneventful Sunday, when I was doing a hit for MSNBC using the NBC studios in northwest Washington. On Sunday mornings, the main function of those studios is the taping of *Meet the Press* with Tim Russert, one of the crown jewels of a network where pecking orders are not unknown. The studios and offices there on Nebraska Avenue have seen a lot of history—the green room walls are adorned with old photos of Adlai Stephenson, Nelson Rockefeller, John Kennedy, and Dave Garroway—but the facilities are ancient and cramped. In those crowded hallways one sometimes runs into the occasional intern giving a gratuitous impression of just how fortunate we cable news droids are merely to be allowed on premises normally sanctified by actual *network broadcasting.* With just the right tone of condescension, one such staffer hooked me up that morning to the audio equipment in an otherwise unpopulated studio, announced that my segment was now floating indefinitely and that they would check with Secaucus to find out what was happening. "Only don't hold your breath. We're really busy doing stuff for all the VIPs in the building."

No problem that the VIPs obviously didn't include me and even the limbo world of the floater was nothing new to me by this point, but being treated like the hired help rankled. An ensuing brain fart wiped out all coherent thought as well as the elementary lessons supposedly internalized before wearing the sound gear into the men's room for the first time. Slipping the surly bonds of self-restraint, I remember muttering some unkind comments about parentage, ancestry, IQ, and maybe even personal hygiene. As Dick Cheney might have put it, I felt somewhat better after venting, and in due course did the hit on MSNBC and left the building.

On the way home, I remembered to switch my cell phone back on and received an urgent message to call the chief booking producer at the network, an estimable lady named Izzie. Such follow-ups after an appearance didn't happen all the time, but it was always nice to be congratulated. "Jackass," she began. In twenty-eight years of military service and two marriages, this was a term I had heard before, but from the affable Izzie it was a bad sign. How could I have said such things, she wanted to know. As she recounted an eerily accurate version of what had been mumbled under my breath in the fool's privacy of a quiet studio, there was no longer any mystery: the mike had been hot all along. In addition to regretting the damage to someone else's feelings—intentional or not—I also felt supremely stupid for making such a rookie mistake. But what do you say? "Sorry, I wasn't really trying to be a jerk, just dumb enough to forget the most basic rule of broadcasting." That seemed like a fairly weak response, and it took all of five seconds to decide that a George Patton-level apology was the better course.

Which I did, complete with flowers sent to everyone involved. Lessons in humility are usually painful as they are useful, but Tim, C.J., and the MSNBC sound crew probably wonder a bit at my odd habit of completely removing the audio gear before going on any potty breaks.

It's mostly about good video

Television being an intensely visual medium, video is the raw material—yea, the mother's milk—of the air factory. Fortunately the daily race to put stuff "on air" is aided and abetted by the exponential growth of the digital revolution. Back when there were only three TV networks—sometime in the seventeenth century according to most high school history students—anyone you saw with a video recorder was apt to be a reporter. But from Rodney King to Abu Ghraib prison, the proliferation of handhelds, digital cameras and even imagery-enabled cell phones amounts to an explosion, and with any luck we'll bring you that explosion even before the smoke has cleared.

It is a different question entirely if good video equals good news, but we really don't care as long as the video is compelling. Ever since the Vietnam War, there has been a recurrent controversy over whether the modern press is capable of covering the many dimensions of war. Some argue that the television era has made it impossible to focus on the "big picture" because it focuses so single-mindedly on bringing you so many little ones, and with the bad news inevitably outweighing the good. It is an open and endlessly fascinating debate, with new case studies generated every day by the conflict in Iraq and the larger backdrop of the "war in the shadows" against terrorism. No final or even tentative answers are suggested here. But there can be little question that a new kind of logic has fallen into place: if war is a contest of the will, then electronic images shape perceptions, perceptions determine the difference between victory and defeat—and even the fundamental choices between war and peace. In the twenty-first century, the keys to these elements—and much else besides—are televised images.

Jim Miklaszewski is NBC's Pentagon correspondent and as an astute observer as there is of the military and the media, especially their sometimes uncomfortable relationship with each other. How good? Well, during the near-constant attacks on Iraq ordered by President Clinton, there were several occasions when Jim's Pentagon sources were good enough for him to suggest precisely when we should be in our chairs up at MSNBC, made up and ready to go. Each time, he was right on the money about what was going down and when. But Jim is equally shrewd at understanding what is *not* going down. To illustrate the small wars of the new century, he had done a superb series of interviews and special features on the drug wars then galvanizing supplier countries like Colombia. Shortly after one of those features aired, I called him with my congratulations, opining as well that U.S. forces were becoming more and more engaged in the drug wars and edging ever closer to wider involvement. But Jim's reply brought me right back to earth: "Nope, there's a built-in limit to our involvement down there: no video." Right again.

Maybe the best example of our video obsession came during that the first winter after 9-11. Governor Tom Ridge—shortly to be secretary of the new Department of Homeland Security—was on TV explaining the new color-coded alert levels. Suddenly in the lower right-hand corner of the screen, we began showing a cut-out of a dog trapped on an ice floe in the nearby Passaic River. Our anchor did a smooth voice-over explaining that this was "a developing situation" that we would be monitoring it even as Governor Ridge went on and on about how alert level Orange might be easily distinguished from Mauve. It took maybe a minute or so for the MSNBC production staff to sense what was happening. Then a number of loud cheers rang out for the dog, though, ominously, none at all for Governor Ridge. As though an applause meter had materialized in the studio, the on-screen picture again shifted, now to a side-by-side shot of the dog and the governor. The governor's affable expression didn't seem to change, but a firefighter could now be seen on a neighboring ice floe inching closer. "Ten dollars on the dog," someone shouted. "Make that twenty," someone else replied, but there were no takers because everyone realized the outcome was no longer in doubt. Within maybe a minute, Governor Ridge had disappeared entirely, and now viewers everywhere had an unobstructed image of Fido, the floes and the firefighter in their watery tableau. "We'll be right back to Governor Ridge," the anchor intoned by way of explanation. "But first, we're following this developing story."

Later, the dog safely rescued and Governor Ridge all but forgotten, I wiped away tears of laughter while rehashing that afternoon's programming choices with Nikki, one of our more experienced and able producers. "I really hated myself for doing that," she admitted. "But Governor Ridge versus live video of a dog being rescued in the river? Oh, please. It would have been a tough decision only if there had been a car chase going on at the same time."

Forget what I just said;
it's really all about ratings

At almost every one of my speeches, someone pops up with a question—although most folks try to be nice—implying that TV news is sometimes, well, superficial. Now these folks or their business associations have paid for me to be there, so I make every effort to be nice. But on these occasions it's sometimes hard to suppress one of the standby expressions of the modern adolescent: "Like DUUUUUH." *Of course* we're superficial! How could it be any other way when every home in America that has cable TV also has a remote control? We know hour by hour, even minute by minute, when the audience is watching us and when they are using those remotes to change the channel to Fox, CNN, or reruns of *Gilligan's Island*. So do our advertisers. They keep us in business and so do you: so put that clicker down 'cause we're bringing you exactly what you asked us for. (And if somehow we aren't, we'll change things in a heartbeat.)

But if you have paid the slightest attention then by now it should be clear that what political scientists call some "fundamental linkages" are at work here. The most basic ones are the programming demands of daily cable news TV and the hunger for compelling video to fill all those hours. But so too is the absolute necessity of getting someone to pay for it, which is where those advertisers come in, and where you do too, because ratings drive everything we do. Small wonder then that car crashes, dogs on ice floes, and "celebrity journalism" can often pre-empt coverage of the weightiest events, even in a country at war. The best producers understand that coverage needs to be carefully balanced between the four basic compass points of TV programming: *the immediate, the compelling, the entertaining, and the important*. When that balance is well honed, the audience approval shows up in higher ratings. But for a long time when I started, it was an article of faith at MSNBC that anything involving international affairs was a death wish for ratings, unless there were other reasons to cover the story.

However, MSNBC nevertheless excelled in covering the spasmodic military adventures of the later Clinton years—from Iraq to Kosovo and back again. But the producers often seemed surprised when their ratings correspondingly went up and regretful but somehow relieved when the "normal" ratings resumed after the shooting stopped. Nowhere along the line did they appear to grasp what Fox clearly understood and exploited even before 9-11: that people instinctively care about the issues of war and peace. So too the corollary: no matter where they come down on those issues, they care just as deeply about the soldiers, sailors, airmen, and marines sent into harm's way. Once that principle was understood, the race for the ratings simply meant giving the audience a good reason to watch us during the war and afterward.

It may be a persistent personal delusion, but during my nine years as an analyst with MSNBC there has always seemed to be an untapped potential for our military coverage. During wars and crises, one sensed that the country was watching what we had to say, if for no other reason than that it was unaffected by spinners in either the networks, the Pentagon, or the White House. Did we have to deal with fickle audiences and sometimes superficial coverage? Sure. But if you look at what all the networks have done, you have to be impressed at the fact that they have invested greater or lesser amounts of time and money in the retired military officers featured throughout this book. All of us strive to bring you "the rest of the story." Meanwhile, both the History and Discovery channels have similarly devoted even more prominence to military subjects, often using some of those same colleagues for backup expertise. It may be that the specialty channels—like the mainstream networks—are reacting in different ways to an increasingly dangerous world. But without those ratings, none of us would enjoy the privilege of being regular guests in your living rooms: it's your way of inviting us in.

Glad to see you, but please don't step on my agenda

The ratings are the ultimate judges of every program and every talent, from anchors to hairdressers, creating an eat-or-be eaten ethos underlying all of TV news. Basically everything is transitory, everyone is constantly jockeying for position, and there is a profound understanding that there is no job security in TV land. The atmosphere is not unlike a line infantry battalion: people tend to be cordial but cautious, and relationships are largely defined by working roles as well as by some incredibly long hours. As in the stock market, there are rewards for success and penalties for failure, so everybody is constantly working some kind of angle: anchor positions, production slots, promotion, retention or transfer schemes, even book deals.

Those angles and agendas change quickly and often; they are rarely written down, but they are absolutely crucial to what goes on in every network. Who's up? Who's down? Who's in? Who's out? Which show is about to be cancelled? While rumors are constant, if you really want to understand what's going on, seek out those makeup artists I told you about in the last chapter. As the comely custodians of beauty in an image-conscious industry, they enjoy confidences shared only with psychiatrists or bartenders anywhere else. So figure out your own agenda, seek out these people and learn their many lessons, and trust me, you do need makeup before going on TV. I quickly swallowed my pride and learned to apply my own makeup in a pinch, which proved to be a surprisingly necessary skill. Vanity can be a strange thing, though, and at least one retired general dismissed out of hand my suggestion that makeup was as necessary in this venue as camouflage had been in our former one. (Then again, he was former Air Force and they aren't great ones for face paint.)

But the other reason to get makeup is that the waiting room—usually known as the green room—is not only an important crossroads but also a great equalizer. It is as if the gods had decreed that Democritus should be in charge of the makeup and hair arrangements, the better to keep everyone humble. As also mentioned in the previous chapter, Patty McLaughlin presides over the makeup department of NBC Capitol Hill studios in an artfully combined role of den mother and traffic cop. Both functions are critical in a place where the usual Washington flotsam and jetsam—congress people, senators, pundits, and panhandlers—have to mix smoothly with us working stiffs. And at odd moments some genuine celebrities can drop in too: Patty has honest-to-God pictures of herself with Archbishop Desmond Tutu and George Clooney.

It is a place of odd bedfellows, where one can encounter both Gordon Liddy and John Dean—the latter in the surreal hours when we were simultaneously covering the impeachment of Bill Clinton and, in a related development, the latest bombings of Baghdad. On one particularly memorable evening, I had separate green room conversations with Dan Quayle and Al Franken, who really is even funnier in person than he is on TV (Al, not Dan). Leaving the studio later, I casually asked our rather buxom receptionist if she had gotten an autograph. "Sure did," she replied, "and the gang thought it was so hilarious that I'm thinking of having it framed. What do you think?"

"Dear Sally," the autograph read, "I can't wait until we have sex again! Al Franken."

I assume she went ahead with the framing, but there was no information volunteered about any Dan Quayle autograph (either content or spelling).

Proactive is not really a word, but it's what you should be if you're smart

One of the first and most useful of all lessons is that complete spontaneity in the world of TV news is something to be avoided at all costs. I learned that painful but useful lesson during my final days in uniform, accepting a hit from a hard-pressed booker who was either a little more devious or a lot less knowledgeable than he seemed on the phone. The interview was a disaster: not only were the questions different, but the only possible answers drifted onto the shoals of classified information. The more the anchor pressed, the more I waffled; it was like running for office in New Jersey. The experience led to a new rule: It's good to answer the question but far better to help write the script. Easy enough to say, but actually doing it meant learning more about the fundamentals of the TV production process, particularly the roles of the producers and the writers. Whether the issue is a military crisis or garden variety celebrity justice, those people tend to ask some fairly basic questions: "What's really going on here?" "Where is this story heading?" And even more critically, "What does our audience want to know about these events?" As President Clinton spawned more military adventures for us to dissect for the electronic audience, there were correspondingly more chances to work more closely with the MSNBC production staff.

After a topic was chosen, we would work with the producers to scope out the issue, to identify who could best discuss it on-air, and even to suggest what the questions might be. Sometimes these preparations had some unintended side effects, like the time one of our producers booked me for an appearance on that evening's show, which was centered on the perennial issue of Army readiness. The Army cares deeply about being ready and able for war to the point of becoming cranky and out of sorts whenever the subject came up. But the producer assured me that the Army was cooperating nicely this time and had already identified the officer who would appear with us. Coincidentally, the general in question was a friend and former colleague from the West Point faculty who had recently been assigned to Pentagon duty. It had been probably ten years, so I contacted his office three times that afternoon to say hello without ever getting through or even past the secretary. The fourth time, an obviously harassed aide picked up the line and said apologetically, "Sir, the general sends his best wishes, but he can't talk." And then in tones suggesting imminent execution, the aide confided, "The boss is up to his ass right now with the public affairs monkeys going over PowerPoints. Poor bastard has to go on TV tonight with Brian Williams." I smiled, remembering my own time on the Army staff when we were beaten every day—good or bad. Eventually my friend came on the line. I explained that the evening's intent was just a five-minute, well-informed conversation and that the battalions of briefing officers could safely be dismissed. That night our hit came off flawlessly, and I'm almost certain the Army staff was able to recycle all those PowerPoint slides.

Beat it to death . . . then turn on a dime

The race for the ratings means that we will stay with a news story—national, local, or whatever—just as long as we think the audience is interested in hearing about it. While we are on it we will also be endlessly inventive about new ways to repackage what you may already know but somehow may have been missed. As we approach a point just short of demonstrable overkill, we will harangue the audience with absurd Questions of the Day designed to stimulate call-in or e-mail responses: for example, Kobe and Michael: Double Standards or Embedded Racism? At almost precisely the point that your hand reaches spasmodically for your remote control—"Ethel, I'm changing that damned channel right *now*"—our coverage shifts seamlessly, and the old story is dispelled like an alarm clock ending a nightmare. *Because there is always, always, always something new.*

Turning on a dime is what every network does and sometimes the choice is easy. In the early spring of 1999, we were in the middle of covering the small but ugly war over Kosovo, which eventually brought me on-air with Geraldo. Compelling video of NATO bombing runs over Belgrade guaranteed virtually round-the-clock coverage—until we started broadcasting some breaking news out of Colorado about a place called Columbine. In the studio that day I had been discussing the NATO bombing with Chris Jansing, a veteran anchor and a valued colleague. The next time I saw her was the following morning but now she was wearing a ski parka, perched in a field adjacent to the high school and doing live interviews with grieving families.

This doesn't tell you everything you need to know about news TV, but it does tell you a lot. Imagine the intellectual agility and the discipline required of an anchor to go out on that kind of assignment at a moment's notice: to drop everything, to change the whole focus of your job, and to go to places where there are often physical risks in covering the news. Many of those same challenges are shared by the reporters, producers, and technicians who usually go along; but doing those things in front of the camera, doing them well, and doing them consistently is something very special. It means you may not have an in-depth knowledge of any issue but that you are an awfully quick study on almost all of them. And while you may differ with your producers and network executives on some things, more typically there is a shared instinct for the guts of the story and how to get it "out there."

But if you consider it a challenge to shift from Kosovo to Columbine over the course of a day, then imagine the double-clutching orgy of improvisation that occurs when the story shifts under your feet, because sometimes it does. So it was on a bright spring day in May 1998 when an urgent phone call summoned me to the NBC studios on Nebraska Avenue in Washington. We were reporting on the vaguely terrifying news that Pakistan had just tested a nuclear weapon. Long before 9-11, it had been an article of faith in the national security community that the Indian subcontinent was one of the most dangerous places on earth. Apart from seething ethnic and religious tensions, more than sixty years of India-Pakistan rivalry had produced unending conflicts that had exploded into shooting wars on at least four—or was it five?—occasions. Just when you thought the neighborhood couldn't get any worse, Pakistan had now joined India in the nuclear club—when investments in water purification and flush toilets seemed far more sensible to Western eyes. But as a Muslim country Pakistan was now in possession of something far more ominous: the dreaded "Islamic bomb."

So where might these things lead? I was mentally going over the answers that might be asked by Brian Williams as part of the special report that was being prepared—even as I was being miked, made up, and escorted to an NBC studio kept sufficiently refrigerated so as to be able in a pinch to double as a meat locker. As I shivered, Brian introduced the program and explained its urgency to the audience. Several senators then came on for a while and spoke reasonably about why nuclear war might not be such a good thing. "Ten minutes, Ken, and then we're coming to you," the producer whispered through my IFB. I nodded silently to the camera in reply. A local NBC reporter stuck his head in to ask where, for their evening broadcast, might they go to tape the reactions of the local Pakistani community. "The Seven-Eleven?" I offered hopefully. The reporter seemed unimpressed and left.

The ten minutes to airtime now were getting down to five. I looked at my notes one more time, cleared my throat, and checked my tie in the monitor. Just in time to see the crawl line on the bottom of the screen: ACTOR PHIL HARTMAN FOUND DEAD IN HOLLYWOOD. There is something startling in the death of any celebrity and like millions of Americans I had enjoyed Hartman's comedy on *Saturday Night Live*. But now I realized that the India-Pakistan confrontation was going nowhere—neither on our network nor hopefully in real life, although the latter was far from guaranteed. Brian Williams never missed a beat and neither did MSNBC; with the old story completely eclipsed by the new, they were more sensitive to my suggestions about frostbite being imminent and soon realized the wisdom of sending me on my way. Plus they probably needed that frigid studio for their next segment.

Sometimes things can get a little ugly

Given the race for the ratings, all the networks cover celebrities: their marriages, divorces, illegitimacies, scandals, arrests, and (inevitably) their departures for the hereafter. But many people remember MSNBC for its coverage of the death of Princess Diana, which occurred shortly after the network went on the air for the first time. First impressions are hard to live down, and for a long time afterward the inside joke around the water coolers and in the cafeteria line was, "You're dead…and we're LIVE ON MSNBC!"

The need to fill airtime every day means that there are lots of other uglies in the news business beyond its coverage of celebrities, often magnified by the phenomenon known as "herd journalism." Because if it seems to you that the networks tend to cover the same stories in many of the same ways, well actually we do. The reason is that during duty hours, our producers sit in the studio functioning essentially as kibitzers, watching banks of monitors tuned to our competition at

CNN and Fox, as well as the major broadcast networks. What any one of them does at any given moment immediately triggers the reaction, "Have you seen what _____ is doing with this story?" Meetings and conference calls are quickly convened and presto, soon there is another electronic demonstration that imitation is the most sincere form of flattery.

Sometimes herd journalism can cascade into bad taste because the war on terror and Iraqi combat routinely produce all kinds of troubling images—flag-draped coffins or hooded prisoners of war (POWs) at the Abu Ghraib prison—that often blur the dividing line between the "public's right to know" and customary limits of taste and good judgment. Even in normal circumstances, reasonable people can easily disagree on where to draw that line, but bad news accompanied by great video can easily stampede the herd. Although that herd now includes Al Jazeera—designated cheerleaders of the jihad—mainstream cable and broadcast outlets have thus far shown commendable self-restraint by banishing beheadings and snuff videos to the netherworld of mosques, madrassas, and Islamist Web sites. Being on their best behavior, however, does not mean that the networks have forgotten for a second what constitutes good TV: conflict and controversy—and the louder the better.

In August 2004, Senator Zell Miller followed up a fiery speech at the Republican National Convention by getting into a nasty confrontation with MSNBC *Hardball* host Chris Matthews, with the senator even regretting on-air that dueling had gone out of fashion. But far from retreating and issuing shame-faced apologies, MSNBC quickly rebroadcast the interview and even inserted excerpts in our promos to show that *Hardball* was more than simply the title of the show.

Those aggressive instincts, never far from the surface, are firmly embedded in the media culture from anchors to the most junior staffers. One day while at the NBC studios in Washington for an unrelated hit, news came over the wire that Senator Barry Goldwater had passed away. I was certainly not a friend but had been a Congressional Fellow when the senate passed a landmark piece of defense legislation subsequently named in the senator's honor. Knowing that a little knowledge at such a moment could be valuable to hard-pressed producers trying to work the story, I quickly jotted down some notes: that this defense legislation had changed American history; that its reforms were critical to the success of the first Gulf War just four years later; and that Senator Goldwater's leadership had been essential at all points. In the newsroom, I grabbed a junior staffer, mentioned the breaking news bulletin and quickly explained that my notes might be helpful in framing the story. Instead he simply stood up, pointed to me and triumphantly shouted to everyone within earshot, "Hey! I've got somebody here who knows the dead guy!"

Don't call them sound bites; think of
them as nuggets of pure gold

The historical and political choices framing the development of Yossi's Gap and the Electronic Coliseum were explained earlier in this book—basic facts of life that even 9-11 and the war on terror have not changed all that much. These sociological underpinnings meant that a lack of military knowledge in the media—and on both sides of the camera—had to be taken for granted. After 9-11, for example, with wars looming in Afghanistan and elsewhere, there was simply no time for reporters, anchors, and producers to revisit the overlooked disciplines of their squandered youth. That situation will probably improve as the latest generation of young journalists is gradually shaped by the discipline of war coverage, and the junior reporters, analysts, and videographers with "embed" experience eventually reach more senior positions. But until that happened, the military analyst was simply thrown into the TV studio as an often imperfect stopgap, or as historian Sir Michael Howard acidly noted, drawn from a cadre of former military officers long and deservedly retired. But sometimes you just have to make do with what you have, recognizing that both the audience and our new media colleagues were operating from a fairly narrow base of military knowledge.

The problem was that the format of most cable TV news rests on the unshakable assumption that the audience has the attention span of a gnat, so the usual hit consisted of no more than three to five minutes in front of the cameras, after which the program shifted breezily and instantly to other topics. Inevitably there was far more to say than time to say it. Even worse, whatever producers or directors were working the story rarely had time for nuances, or sometimes even the basics. As a result, our segments sometimes seemed as hastily composed as a painter executing a portrait under the pressure of a thirty-second shot clock. To avoid leaving the audience with caricatures of reality, certain recurring phrases had a way of turning up in these on-air improvisations: "Brian this is only a first report and we should remember that the first reports in war are usually wrong." Or "Lester, we're making a lot out of these air attacks, but what really matters is the integration of air, ground, and even sea forces." Or even more eerily, "Chris, those precision-guided munitions are certainly an impressive display of American technological sophistication, but let's remember that this low-tech enemy will eventually get a vote here too."

We sometimes referred to it as "succinctitude" and no one was better at it than Gen. Mick Trainor, a close friend and probably the only Marine in all of recorded military history to have later become not only the Pentagon correspondent of the *New York Times* but also a Harvard professor. Other former flag officers were occasionally run through the studios for a weekend audition just as I had been, but some of them clearly struggled to adjust to the abrupt rat-a-tat-tat of a three-minute interview. You had to understand that they had fought their way to the top of the military profession, and having become warlords, had also become used to having their every utterance treated with scriptural reverence; it must have now seemed like blasphemy to deal with a twenty-something segment pro-ducer intent on reducing everything to a three-minute hit that just might run short. Dave Murphy is a bearded, no-nonsense assistant producer who has been an MSNBC stalwart for most of my time with the network. "Geez, what was wrong with that guy?" Dave asked me after one particularly painful appearance by a former general who had shown up carrying a suit bag with his name and rank embroidered in gold. I tried to explain, relating the following story. One of my friends had been speechwriter to a four-star Army general who had once administered a more-severe-than-usual ass chewing when his remarks seemed to have left one audience several millimeters short of "wildly enthusiastic." The text of the ass chewing was that any deficiency was clearly the sole responsibility of the speechwriter, who up until that point was considered so reliable that the gen-eral seldom even bothered to proof the text prior to delivery. Next time out, as my friend gleefully described it, he heard the general intone these words exactly as written: "I am not only *happy* to be here with you but am indeed *glad*."

The occasional war college professor who wound up on our air deserved more sympathy because the careful nuances and cautious phrasings appropriate to the *McNeil-Lehrer News Hour* had to be jettisoned in the near food fight of a three-cornered debate with rapid-fire anchors like John Gibson, later a Fox News star and the only one who ever quizzed me about Herodotus. "My God," gasped one of my former comrades-in-arms after such an experience. "This *definitely* ain't PBS!" Indeed it wasn't, but we struck new blows for brevity during the 2003 invasion of Iraq with the "military minutes" that aired twice an hour during MSNBC's extended programming. No matter, with pointers and a glib phrase or two, there were no maneuvers or engagements so complex that we couldn't over-simplify them in fifty-five seconds, sometimes right on the mark too. And then it was back to you....

It was exhausting, with eight-hour shifts and multiple hits that left you drained and sometimes incapable of even forming complete sentences. During these times of great stress and extended programming, the mysterious folkways of the book-ers brought into our midst some new analytical blood, recently retired, clearly well qualified as military experts, but touchingly naïve when it came to joining in our reindeer games. Today's professional military has few members who could not be fairly characterized as "hard chargers": thus one of our new colleagues eagerly accepted a producer's invitation to suggest how an upcoming segment might be organized. Frankly, we were looking for almost any fresh thoughts at that point: we were dead tired and had already said several times everything that could conceivably be said about how the war was going. Reaching into his military-issue briefcase, Marv (*not* his real name) pulled out some briefing notes about "combat priorities" he had written for the last general for whom he had served.

"How 'bout this?" he offered, turning the pages rapidly.

"a. A is for Army. We're the Army. Hoaaaaahhhhh!"

"b. B is for Battles. The Army wins the nation's battles."

"c. C is for Combat. Combat is our highest priority."

By this point the producer had an expression on her face suggesting she had posed for that famous painting, *The Scream*. "Ummmmmmmm. I just don't think we'll be going in that direction on this segment," she said as she hurried off. We commiserated briefly with Marv, who was not invited back after his rotation ended.

What we're not supposed to say

If you are reading this expecting to get the inside skinny on media bias on either side of the political spectrum, read no farther. Are those biases there? Yes, of course, so what else is new? Consider just some of the basics: intelligent people generally have strong opinions; if you aren't smart and opinionated, you probably shouldn't be anywhere close to the media; and as long as you're up front about what those opinions are, so what? Most of us believe that CNN leans a little to the left, Fox News to the right, and at MSNBC we figure we have done our jobs if we get criticized by both sides.

Call it luck, or just trying to play things straight up, regardless of who was in office at the time, but in almost nine years with MSNBC, I have never yet been told my views on any given subject were politically unacceptable to the network. No one from either of the last two administrations has ever—to my knowledge—complained to the NBC leadership about my on-air comments, although the Clintonistas had grounds and the Pentagon—no matter who is in charge—really does know how to hold a grudge. But it's not Left versus Right, Democrat versus Republican politics that you have to watch out for; instead it's the network version of good old office politics that can do you in. Individual program hosts like Don Imus, Chris Matthews, or Joe Scarborough have their own views, which is a major part of the reason why they have their own shows to start with. Their opinions are inevitably reflected in what gets said and, more important, who gets invited to appear on their shows. How do those choices get made? Pretty much a combination of the personal preferences and agendas driven by the show's host together with what the invited guest can do to advance a given story and maybe to help boost ratings.

Like the weather, those bookings come and go. For several years after 9-11, I became something of a regular on Don Imus's program, which is a little like getting orders to a combat zone. "I'd rather get shot again than go on with that SOB," was how one of my military colleagues once expressed his feelings. Sir John Gielgud expressed the same thought more elegantly in the movie *Arthur*: "Normally one would have to go to a bowling alley to meet such people." For a little while I was actually considered one of the Imus gang until he apparently became disaffected either with me or my views on the war in Iraq. When the exhilaration of the war's initial victories morphed into the considerably grimmer reality of occupation, insurgency, and American casualties, my appearances on the show decreased and eventually stopped altogether. That's just the way it is, or as Imus himself often puts it, "Don't write, don't call. If we want you, we'll call *you*." On Imus and similar shows there is often a perceived need to go to "fresh faces" from time to time, particularly when the editorial emphasis shifts, and by this time Imus was regularly referring to the Bush/Cheney/Rumsfeld team as war criminals. (Although he characteristically recanted when Cheney agreed to make a pre-Inaugural appearance on the show in January 2005.)

Living well is the best revenge, and my successor on the show was Col. Jack Jacobs, a good friend and West Point colleague who had been awarded the Medal of Honor in Vietnam. In real life, Jack is an investment banker but he sometimes puts down one of his two cell phones long enough to make the odd appearance on MSNBC, always with a constant undertone of hilarity that seems not all that far removed from vaudeville. He once convulsed Barry McCaffrey and me with the following story:

> McCaffrey and Jacobs are sitting in a bar and Jacobs says, "I think my wife is dead." McCaffrey replies, "Whaddya mean you think your wife is dead? What kind of thing is that to say?" Jack responds, "Well, the sex is about the same, but the laundry's piling up." (Rimshot offstage)

Part of the reason for his on-air success—banking is another matter entirely—is that Jack's Vietnam combat experience became especially important when the Iraqi insurgency became an unexpected throwback to classic guerrilla warfare.

Nothing tougher to talk about, but Jack does it the way soldiers often do to relieve the tension—with a sardonic, Gary Larson style of humor. One of those moments came when we were doing a one-year retrospective marking the invasion of Iraq. Brian Williams was hosting the special and moderating a panel composed of Gen. Wayne Downing and Gen. Barry McCaffrey teamed with Jack and me. One of Brian's questions dealt with mistakes: With the benefit of hindsight, what might American forces have done differently? Jack never hesitated: "I think we learned about the downside of our psychological operations. Like fools, we scattered thousands of leaflets telling the Iraqis to lay down their weapons, abandon their positions and live on to fight another day. They did as we asked and the insurgency there today is partly the result: we would have been better off killing them when we had the chance."

The old soldiers all suppressed a collective giggle at this sudden outburst of truth while Brian moved on as smoothly as ever. But Jack had illuminated a subject often overlooked in discussions about the vagaries of "national security policy": that war is the defining act of those policies and that war necessarily involves killing the enemy. This is rough stuff for media executives painfully attuned to the political correctness of every utterance. And even the Army, always alert to the tender sensibilities of its civilian masters, had occasionally been tempted by doublespeak; during the Cold War, we had even borrowed the systems analysis term "target servicing," not only as a kinder, gentler term for killing but also to put a patina of science on what is essentially a bloody slug fest.

But as long as we don't make a habit of it we can occasionally get away with soldier talk, and don't bring more gore into the living rooms of the audience than what they're already used to from, let's say, watching *The Sopranos*. But we treasure the odd foray into the enemy territory of political correctness, and especially prize those who have crossed the line and lived to tell the tale. Not surprisingly, Jack Jacobs is the all-time winner, largely on the strength of a memorable appearance with Alex Witt, our weekend anchor and a great lady with a wicked sense of humor all her own. Alex's other guest that morning was Lt. Col. Rick Francona, another of our other military analysts and a genuine Arab expert in his own right.

Naturally, the topic was the insurgency in Iraq and Rick had briefly outlined how the deep ethnic divisions of that country were contributing to a rising guerrilla movement. Deadly dull stuff, of course, but this is where Jack jumped to the rescue, just after Alex had asked him about cross-border Iranian involvement with the Shi'ite minority in the south. Gesturing at the map, Jack said, "Yes, Alex, that's a real problem because in the area down south here around Basra, because they just have a whole *pile* of Shi'ites to deal with." Jack had a characteristically deadpan expression as he uttered those words, but there was no mistaking the look that instantly flashed across Alex's face. Yes, the double entendre meaning behind "pile of Shi'ites" had fully struck home: now the question was whether composure could be maintained until the end of the segment. Knowing the people involved, I was betting on an explosion of laughter from all three of them just before Alex could gasp, "We'll be right back after these important messages," and then fall out of her chair once the cameras were clear.

Amazingly enough, it didn't happen. On air, Alex maintained the seasoned calm of a professional anchor, Jack never cracked a smile and Rick Francona could easily have passed for the polished military diplomat he once was. But both Alex and Rick admitted later that this was definitely one of "those" moments and they had indeed come close to losing it. And Jack? Well, he admits to nothing and even insists that nothing ever happened, a phrase his friends have often heard him use before. Jack earned the respect and honor of his countrymen by being awarded the Medal of Honor, but among his colleagues, it was the "pile of Shi'ites" that truly made him a legend.

CHAPTER FOUR

A New Kind of War

• • • • •

T he contract and retainer agreement with MSNBC was nice because it not only compensated my on-camera appearances but also covered the time spent behind them—consultations that were becoming more frequent. One morning in October 2000 I heard our anchor Greg Jarrett delivering the matter-of-fact announcement that an American naval vessel had apparently suffered an explosion while anchored at a port outside Yemen, and that the vessel was one of the Navy's latest. A quick call to our news desk revealed that the ship, which turned out to be the USS *Cole*, was an Aegis-class destroyer, a state-of-the-art vessel designed to be the eyes and ears of the fleet in the supposedly high-tech naval wars of the twenty-first century. Yet it had not been able to foresee an attack carried out by a very low-tech enemy, probably suicide bombers in a small boat. After reaching Jarrett several minutes later, I quickly explained that the attack on the USS *Cole* was likely to be a huge story, that it was an excellent example of how a weaker force could take on a stronger adversary, that attacks on American naval vessel were exactly the sort of thing that had started wars all the way from the Barbary Pirates to Pearl Harbor and that this was a bold, in-your-face assault by an adversary who presumably understood this history. This was of course far more information than any anchor could possibly have used at just that moment, but it might help to define an otherwise ambiguous situation when everything else was suddenly fluid.

Backstopping like that for breaking news was something every military analyst did on every network; it was one of the main reasons why the news folks occasionally found it useful to have us hanging around. But sometimes a really interesting project came along that you could really get your teeth into. MSNBC regularly produces its own documentaries as part of its *MSNBC Investigates* series and one raw January day I negotiated a recent Washington snowfall to tape a segment for one of their projects. The producer explained how they had been increasingly drawn to the issue of terrorism and were now wondering if terrorists might be audacious enough to attack the American homeland. I nodded sagely and said that the pattern was clear. The attacks on the USS *Cole* and the twin bombings of the American embassies in Africa were surrogates. All were sovereign American territory and represented a willingness to hit us anywhere—including the United States—with whatever means might be at hand. The producer pressed on: How about attacking New York City? I outlined some speculative theories, including attacks against American nuclear power plants, based on research done several years earlier. After a half-hour of taping, I left but throughout that year regularly made it a point to check in with the producer to see how they were doing. By late August, the special still had not aired, the producer explaining that they had unearthed far more material than they could use. However, taping was now complete, editing nearly so, and some "really cool" animation prepared showing a "dirty bomb" being detonated at the World Trade Center. The special, titled *Attack on Manhattan*, was now scheduled for an air date sometime in the next month: September 2001.

For obvious reasons, the program did not actually air until a year later when the shock had somewhat lessened, and then only as an after-the-fact retrospective to show that the analysts had at least been right if not especially prophetic. Intelligence officers are rightly skeptical of prophecies because most of us are conscious of our own limitations as prognosticators and devoutly prefer to predict the past. Even so, you might think that having been somewhat focused on a terrorist attack against New York, I would have been a little quicker to put things together when the real thing happened. Fact is, I was goofing off, lulled into somnolence by our constant coverage of shark attacks on Florida bathers and the search for missing Washington intern Chandra Levy. The phone rang shortly before nine on that bright fall morning when the sky seemed to sparkle. It was Alla Lora, MSNBC's senior booking producer. "Are you watching our air right now?" she asked. "Ummmmmmmm…actually no, but let me turn the set on. Wow. What just happened?" As Alla quickly explained that a plane had just hit the World Trade Center, my mind reached back, not to the terrorism special, but absurdly to the wacko parachutist we had shown the week before getting hung up on the nearby Statue of Liberty. Surely this was something similar, some mindless stunt with a private plane gone horribly wrong.

Alla replied that there were reports that a commercial airliner was somehow involved, but there was as yet no video to replay showing its actual impact—just the smoke and flames we were seeing now. "That doesn't seem to make much sense either," I replied. "The landing patterns at La Guardia and Newark keep aircraft miles away from those skyscrapers. And just look at the weather. It's as clear up there as it is down here, so even if the pilot had an instrument malfunction...." Just as I said those words, the camera caught the shark-like silhouette of a large jetliner approaching the Twin Towers, and the next instant the towers exploded into a fireball of smoke and debris. It was a kamikaze nightmare lifted from a war movie and the phone almost dropped from my hand. After a minute or so, the power of speech returned. When it did, I told Alla that I was heading for the NBC studios in northwest Washington, would be there within a half hour, and then raced to get ready.

Sometimes the faster you try to move, the slower everything seems. By the time I was on the road, the traffic had noticeably worsened, jamming even my infallible back-door route over the Chain Bridge between McLean and northwest Washington. While I was waiting for a light to change, the radio broadcast another aftershock: a third plane had hit the Pentagon. I had memories of several spectacular visits to the Windows on the World restaurant atop the World Trade Center, but the Pentagon was even more personal, the place where I had worked for four years and where many friends still did. As I crossed the bridge, I looked south down the Potomac River gorge and saw the smoke and flames from the Pentagon were already smudging the horizon. There was no way to be sure, but one knew that people were either dying or in deadly peril at that very instant. My heart sank recalling a conversation the day before with NBC's Pentagon correspondent Jim Miklaszewski. His office was close to the building's Mall entrance. Where had the plane hit and was he OK?

Almost as soon as I ran into the NBC studios Jim's voice could be heard on the air, alive and well but reporting from the burning headquarters that had suddenly become an engagement zone in a war that had often been talked about but never really imagined. Later word came of other friends who had experienced even closer calls. Army Maj. Gen. Bob Wood, a friend since our days together as West Point instructors, had been on the phone comforting his daughter in the aftermath of the New York attacks when the plane hit close to his office. Instantly catapulted to the opposite wall, Bob and his colleagues had to break down doors to escape the flames.[1] One of my former Georgetown students, Maj. Lincoln Leibner, was an Army Green Beret scheduled for a later shift, but his first reaction after seeing the strikes at the World Trade Center was to report immediately to his Pentagon office. On his way in from an adjacent parking lot, Linc witnessed the final seconds of Flight 77 before its fiery impact. He remembers staring at the crash site for several seconds before running toward a building others were rapidly fleeing. As he later told me, "I ran toward the building because that was what I was supposed to do." Moving debris while dodging smoke and flames, he saved the lives of at least three people before being ordered out of the building and narrowly escaping the col-of that section's facade. A member of the secretary's personal staff, he may have been the first to tell Donald Rumsfeld that they had been hit not by a cruise missile or a car bomb but by a commercial airliner.[2]

My own duties now were not nearly so heroic. For the rest of that very long day, I sat in front of the cameras and tried to put unreasonable events into some sort of reasonable context, which was tough to do when other cameras were constantly showing the carnage in New York and Washington. My emotions escaped only once, when NBC anchor Tom Brokaw asked how long it might be before the terrorists were brought to justice. A reasonable question, of course, and similar to those customarily posed after terrorist outrages of one kind or another over much of the last decade. But today's events seemed to require something different: a clearer understanding that *fatwas* (Islamic declarations of holy war) followed by repeated attacks on U.S. embassies, ships, and now the American homeland should be treated not just as crimes but as acts of war requiring a full military response. Even so, my answer was probably a little over the top for someone who now carried the supposedly objective credentials of the analyst: "Tom, we don't need to bring these people to justice, we need to send them to hell."

The adrenaline was still pumping when I left the NBC studios that evening at dusk. Two visible symbols showed just how much the world had changed since morning. The flag that proudly greeted VIPs arriving for television interviews now flew at half-staff; and in one of the busiest air corridors in the nation, the only airplanes visible were a pair of F-15 fighters flying a combat air patrol mission. Other and more subtle changes had occurred as well. On cable news, defense, foreign policy, and hard-core military issues had suddenly gone from being occasional fill-in fare to our latest stock in trade. In the immediate aftermath of the attacks, our coverage went into overdrive to feed viewers ravenous to understand what had just happened and how the United States might respond. At such moments, standard MSNBC practice was to bring the whole gaggle of analysts en masse to the Secaucus studios—the better to spread out the extended in-house coverage. But with Washington's National Airport closed, the airlines grounded, and all other transportation scrambled up and down the east coast, the easy two-hour commute to Secaucus was no longer possible.

Worse yet, the extended programming meant extended hours for all of us, with every available Washington studio pressed into service. Sometimes this meant spending solitary hours in spaces that amounted to little more than particularly well-lit storage closets with only a camera, an earpiece and (maybe) a monitor for company. Whenever this happened, it was a sure bet that overstressed producers back in New Jersey were simply winging it, making up the programming as they went along, and sometimes forgetting that you were even there. When your turn came and the sequence actually aired, there was precious little to indicate if the hit had been right, wrong, or indifferent. There were no studio audiences, of course, or even much in the way of external cues; the overworked technical crew was usually busy handling feeds from several different studios. Unless the terminally bored analyst had gone rogue and suddenly disrobed as a final act of protest (and the thought *did* enter my mind several times) the most feedback you could usually expect from them was a nodded acknowledgment: "Well, the signal looked okay when it left here, Colonel."

Toward the end of that terrible week, seats on the trains became available and the Newark Amtrak station provided my first look at the heart-wrenching photographs of missing relatives from the World Trade Center posted on the station walls. The dreaded first glimpse of lower Manhattan, still smoke shrouded and now shorn of the Twin Towers, brought the expected tears. In contrast, the arrival at MSNBC "World Headquarters" was like a homecoming rally for the football team. Because it is a medium where "cool" is one of the defining virtues, an aura of matter-of-fact nonchalance usually prevails around the studios of MSNBC and most other television studios—but not this time. Now there were hugs, handshakes, backslaps, and congratulations—apparently those broom-closet hits had appeared far better on the receiving end than from their origin at the bottom of the bird cage. There was no question, however, that the twenty-somethings comprising the bulk of the MSNBC family were operating under great stress. For reasons outlined in the preceding chapters, they had no personal acquaintance with war or even serious conflict. But now they had been hit on their doorsteps by conflict in one of its ugliest and most elemental forms. It was affecting them on and off the job—in fact during each of their waking hours.

As so often before, there were a great many blanks to be filled in as the earth shifted and our coverage scrambled to adjust. Mercifully, the trains continued to run on time and we settled into a more or less regular in-studio rotation of military analysts, most of us shuttling back and forth between Washington and Secaucus while continuing to do hits from both locations. A week or so later, I was scheduled to go back to New Jersey, the bookers acquiring coveted space on an express train calculated to minimize travel time while other coverage was in progress. "Now, Bush will be addressing a joint session of Congress about the war on terrorism while you're on the train," one of them explained. "And when you get here, we have you scheduled to sit in with Brian Williams on a wrap-up special he's anchoring. But don't worry: the car service will bring you directly here so there will be plenty of time to see the videotape before you go on." Sounded reasonable, and we had done similar things many times in the past.

Unfortunately, it is at just such times that Murphy's Law disrupts the most carefully crafted plans: the car service charged with collecting me became greatly confused by the assonant similarities of the names "Newark" and "New York" and went to one place while I waited in the other. Mistakes having been made, the result was that evening I walked into the MSNBC studios just in time to throw on the sound equipment, get zapped by the makeup lady with her powder puff and take my seat opposite Brian Williams just before he went live. Brian fixed me with his usual penetrating anchor stare and began framing his question. Luckily, it was prefaced with a series of dependent and independent clauses that gave me valuable time to collect my thoughts, because this was going to take BS to an entirely new level. He finished and looked at me expectantly, not knowing that I had heard neither him nor President Bush. I nodded confidently and plunged ahead: "Brian, listening to President Bush this evening, one could only be reminded of what that master Prussian strategist Clausewitz called the Great Trinity of the War, the People and the Army. Here tonight George Bush justified the war he called for in the immediate aftermath of 9-11. He did so in the People's House, before a joint session of the Congress, because Congress is the war-making body in our system of government. And finally, the president was taking his place tonight at the head of the Army as its commander-in-chief. All in all, a stirring speech and a masterful performance."

Well now, it must have been a good guess because Brian went back and forth for several minutes scoring its major points before moving on to the reactions from other distinguished observers who had a clear advantage over me because they had actually *heard* the speech. Fortunately everyone seemed to agree that the tie-in to Clausewitz was exactly the right way to put it. After about twenty more minutes, the dialogue moved on and one of the producers cleared me off the set; there wasn't much of a chance to do more than nod at Brian as I was leaving. We didn't see each other again for several days, but finally crossed paths in the parking lot one afternoon, shaking hands, talking about the emotions of covering 9-11 and speculating about what it all might mean. As he turned to go into the building, Brian—class guy that he always is—made it a point to congratulate me on what he said had been a great interview after the president's speech. I thanked him but rather meekly added that it was only right to tell him the truth about having missed it entirely. When he realized that I really wasn't kidding, Brian doubled over with a roar of laughter, gave me a high five and shouted, "By God, we'll make a journalist out of you yet!" It's still one of my favorite memories of a real journalist who deserves his success. And, like I said, a class act.

Even as MSNBC was scrambling to adjust to the new environment, our crosstown rivals at the upstart Fox News Network were also trying to figure out their next moves. From the start, Fox had seen itself as the new kid on the block and, led by the brilliant and combative Roger Ailes, one with a definite chip on its shoulder. Already there had been defections: the lineup at Fox was studded with MSNBC alums and old friends like John Gibson, Brigit Quinn, Patty Anne Brown, and Laurie Dhue. Maj. Gen. Paul Vallely is a retired Army infantry officer and former division commander who maintains strong ties to Fort Bragg and the special operations community. Like many of us, he had steadily accumulated a growing portfolio of media experience, mostly quick-reaction hits to breaking news stories on Fox and CNN. On 9-11, Fox caught up with him on a business trip to Atlanta, hastily arranged his return by car to Washington, where he was immediately dragooned into exactly the same kind of intense coverage we were experiencing at that moment. Since the NBC and Fox studios on Capitol Hill are in the same building, it was not unusual for us to run into each other in the elevator and chuckle over the fact that we were now rivals.

Although Paul had never thought of himself as a "TV kind of guy," he had done enough uncompensated freelancing to understand that the cable news business lived and died by the One-Night-Stand Rule: that if they like you, then they invite you back. But the aftermath of 9-11 was wholly new terrain and when senior Fox producers were astute enough to ask him how they might adjust, Paul journeyed to corporate headquarters in New York to tell them. True to his training, he began with the basics: a "war room" was needed that would be both "audience friendly" and also allow the Fox staff and their military analysts to keep track of what was going on in the midst of fast-breaking news. As with any "tactical operations center," maps, briefing boards, and simple graphics would be essential accoutrements. Second only to that requirement was the need to select that best on-camera talent among the military analysts, put them under contract and then pay them for their services. ("Then you mean we're actually going to get *paid* for all this?" shouted an incredulous Bob Scales, normally the most affable and mild mannered of all modern major generals, when he heard the news.)

Indeed they should, as Paul carefully explained to the Fox executives. The era of uncompensated military analysts had ended with the 9-11 attacks. All the networks were now in competition to see who could best cover this story and there was a limited supply of bona fide military experts who were (a) available, (b) articulate, (c) not under contract to anyone else, and (d) still in their right minds. Paul's concept was that this group not be limited to retired generals but that it should also include a balance of ranks and experience, particularly from the special operations community that specialized in using senior noncommissioned officers. Air Force Lt. Gen. Tom McInerny (whom you have already met) and Bob Scales (military historian and former commandant of the Army War College) were two of the first and most obvious hires; but they eventually included Lt. Col. Bill Cowan, USMC (Ret.), and Sgt. Maj. Steve Greer, USA (Ret.)

This group quickly set about educating Fox analysts, producers, and anchors about what possibly lay ahead in Afghanistan. Sometimes it was the small things that needed to be addressed first, like the troubling tendency of an on-air announcer to mangle military ranks. When one is addressing a Lieutenant Commander, for example, it is appropriate to give his or her title in full; thereafter, the higher rank is used. "This is Lieutenant Commander Jeffrey Smith of the U.S. Navy. Good morning, Commander Smith." One Fox anchor had a nasty habit of properly introducing Paul as Major General Vallely, but thereafter referring to him as "Major." Paul made sure the Fox people understood that those kinds of simple errors demonstrated to the audience that only the uniformed participant in the interview was the real professional. Another key function of the military analysts was breaking in the new hires. Because the coin of the realm was the ability to perform on-camera, the Fox and MSNBC experiences were almost identical: rank was simply not a reliable indicator of success in predicting on-camera performance. Some high-ranking officers proved surprisingly inarticulate or, even worse, boring; still others were reluctant to engage in the hurly-burly of cable news or even to go on public record. Meanwhile, Bill Cowan and Steve Greer were becoming stalwarts of Fox coverage.

The network had obviously taken Paul's other advice seriously because Fox analysts were now going on air with noticeably better maps and graphics packages. Barely a month after 9-11 American bombing began in Afghanistan. Shortly thereafter I watched in envious admiration as Tom McInerny narrated a sophisticated graphics sequence illustrating how a laser-guided bomb might be used to attack Taliban hideouts concealed deep in the cave complexes of the world's most mountainous terrain. Screen-writers were added as well, giving the analysts the ability to illustrate their remarks with graphics symbols—doing for military operations what John Madden customarily did for *Monday Night Football*. However, caution was needed because some analysts adjusted better than others to the delicate touch required by the screen-writer—essentially a wide-screen TV with the sensitivity of a touch pad. Military map symbols could be pre-loaded, and as the analyst spoke, a single touch of the screen would cause those symbols to appear instantly. All of us would eventually have screen-writer adventure stories: a typical one occurred when one of the new guys at Fox slapped the screen a little too vigorously and the symbol for a tank division popped up, but now magically accompanied by eight others. In itself, it's not a big deal, but the officer was so startled by this unexpected electronic apparition that he instinctively reverted to soldier-speak and blurted out on-air, "Aw shit!" which actually *was* sort of a big deal.

As the winter of 2001 loomed, Fox joined every other network in gearing up for what everyone assumed would be a long war in Afghanistan. More military analysts were added to the staff, and although the old crowd helped break in the new, they were not always involved in hiring and vetting decisions. The One-Night-Stand Rule had become instinctive and often the new analyst would simply be hired and thrown into the mix whenever openings occurred. In two instances, this failure to check credentials more thoroughly led to televised appearances by two imposters. The first, a "General Disney" was hired because of his distinguished mien, stature as a brigadier in the "Vermont Militia," and textbook knowledge of Afghan caves. The second, Lt. Col. Joseph Cafasso, had a law degree, the Silver Star, and was a veteran of the abortive Iranian hostage raid known as "Desert One."

Things began coming unglued when the real analysts noticed that Disney's specialized knowledge of Afghan caves had been acquired while serving as a U.S. military attaché in the Kabul embassy, but long after it had been closed following the Soviet invasion. The optimism of Colonel Cafasso clearly outran his judgment when he padded an already inflated résumé with supposed service as Paul Vallely's chief of staff. "Hunh?" said Paul, and then the game was pretty much up. "General Disney" vanished as mysteriously as he had come while "Colonel" Cafasso turned out to have just five weeks of military service to his credit, having dropped out of basic training at that point.[3]

Aside from the additional duty of unfrocking the odd imposter, the real importance of the Warheads was that the new kind of war demanded distinctly different departures from conventional journalism, if for no other reason than that conventional journalists had little idea what was going on as the American war machine took dead aim at Afghanistan. Even if they did, a "loose lips sink ships" mentality had suddenly taken hold in an America badly shaken by the terrorist attacks. As American planes and ships closed in on the Afghan periphery from all points of the compass, Greg Jarrett took to prefacing our hits together with a standard caveat: "What we are going to tell you about next comes from information given to us by the Pentagon *knowing that we were going to give it to you*. And while we welcome your calls and e-mails, let me assure you that we are at MSNBC are *not* committing any breaches of national security." In spite of all that Greg probably need not have bothered since we continued to get angry protests from viewers that we were giving away the farm—my favorite being from a retired Coast Guard reservist accusing me of selling out to the media for "big bucks."

Would that it had been true, but in reality the military analysts were only slightly ahead of the journalists in understanding what might be about to happen in the war on terror. As always the Pentagon was being extremely guarded in its comments, putting out a wealth of material that seemed impressive but revealed little. If pressed, they darkly hinted that enough was enough and that anything more might violate operational security. We had now come full circle: one of the Pentagon's immediate reactions to the first Gulf War had been a heightened understanding that the proliferation of media—digital, video, imagery, and most of all, twenty-four-hour television—meant that old notions of "public affairs" had vanished.

In their place was the new doctrine of information operations, which began with the objective of getting inside the news cycle—a goal every bit as important as penetrating the enemy's decision cycle, in turn the key to his or her mind and will. Nor was this something as crude as managing or manipulating the news; in fact the assumption was that the proliferation of media made such simplistic objectives impossible. Instead the idea was to seize and maintain the initiative in telling one's own story while countering any negatives. The new doctrine was not limited to Republican administrations. During the war over Kosovo, for example, I had repeatedly suggested to the MSNBC top brass that moving without pause between back-to-back Pentagon, State Department, and NATO briefings effectively meant ceding hours of uncritical coverage to the government. The network seemed curiously untroubled: they had a lot of airtime to fill each day, ratings were good, and that was that.

If the doctrine of information operations was new, then it rested on a much older premise: the importance of networks. All of us had those personal linkages, of course, and they predated the Internet—some of us grousing that ours were older than the telephone as well. There was no question, however, that lifetimes of personal and professional contacts in and around the military had been made considerably more efficient by the advent of e-mail, electronic bulletin boards, chat rooms, and blogs. All of us maintained those linkages, but the general officer Old Boy Networks were in a class by themselves. When well-connected and well-wired leaders like Bob Scales and Tom McInerny joined Paul Vallely over at Fox it sent precisely the same signal we at NBC had earlier received from generals like Mick Trainor, Barry McCaffrey, and Wayne Downing. It was as if all our respective Old Boy Networks had been recalled to active duty and would now be used to figure out what was really going on—quite independent of official Pentagon sources, news "releases," and spin. Although all of us were independent and back in full possession of our First Amendment rights, we were also part of an extended service family: we reached a Silent Consensus that eventually came to embrace all the military analysts. Using our personal contacts and knowledge, we would seek out the essential military facts bearing on the news, make our own judgments, check our own sources, and occasionally perform sanity checks for each other when the competition for a story permitted it. If such things were relative, then the second part of the Silent Consensus was absolute: We would never knowingly jeopardize the integrity of a military mission or endanger the lives of our comrades-in-arms *even if that meant withholding news or even operationally sensitive information.*

Had they known or cared about the Warheads or our Silent Consensus, the purists in any journalism school would have been quick to object on the grounds of the public's sacred right to know. This would have been OK with us too because we would have been equally quick to dismiss their objections, which ran counter to what we saw good journalists doing every day while working their own sources. Deep and enduring friendships had been formed with our new media colleagues but "media objectivity" came well after the fact that we were still soldiers—first, last, and always. This meant being true to our fellow soldiers and always trying to protect them as a first responsibility. Our cut at "media objectivity" meant remembering that we were no longer obligated by our oaths of political obedience to either party. Instead, the families of those soldiers had a right to expect that on TV we would always "call it as we see it" regardless of who was the commander-in-chief, or whose ox might be gored.

If such attitudes seemed like a sensible way to approach the "war in the shadows" that now loomed in Afghanistan, then reality was shortly to demonstrate just how little we really knew. Barely two months into the campaign, hints had emerged that American forces were doing more than merely bombing Taliban targets. Pentagon-released video on one occasion showed a nighttime Ranger raid descending onto a "suspected Taliban headquarters," but the raid apparently ended with little to show for the action. All of which made the Warheads wonder what was really going on, simply because we had been schooled in the basics of operations security and psychological operations. The way we figured it: if they were releasing Ranger videos it was almost certain that the real action was elsewhere.

Which was where things stood one afternoon in early December while I was in the midst of a regular rotation up at MSNBC: a story surfaced that gave us a sudden and unforgettable insight into what was actually occurring in Afghanistan. As usual, there was no prior warning and the immediate task—to act as an "anchor buddy" during our coverage of a press conference—carried no hint of its ultimate significance. The anchor in question was my buddy Rick Sanchez, now with CNN but at the time one of our "go-to guys" for human interest stories. The press conference was originating from an army medical center in Landstuhl, Germany, where several wounded soldiers had arrived after being air-evaced from

Afghanistan. What was generating press interest in the first place was that their wounds had been sustained when an air strike had gone horribly awry—and a friendly fire story was irresistible amidst the prevailing line of American hi-tech weaponry visiting devastation upon the Hottentots. But the story didn't turn out quite that way and in a very few moments I suddenly found myself face-to-face with Capt. Jason Amerine, an Army Green Beret who looked as if he had been sent over from Central Casting.

He had been wounded in the air strike, but with no hint of bravado, seemed to dismiss the wounds as inconsequential. Instead he coolly took the microphone and apologized for having just arrived in Landstuhl, but he had been delayed by the need to escort the remains of two of his soldiers who had been killed. While acknowledging the sacrifices his team had made, even at the cost of two lives lost, Captain Amerine was determined that this press conference not be dominated by the recitation of a friendly fire incident; his soldiers were heroes rather than victims and their gallantry in combat was the only real story worth telling. At that moment, having smoothly redefined the reason we were all watching him, the captain had the absolutely undivided attention of everyone in the room at Landstuhl. Back in the studio, I turned off my mike, grabbed the producer, and whispered urgently, "Screw the commercials, screw the network. Don't you *dare* break away from this!" Rick Sanchez nodded in agreement and we turned back to the screen where Captain Amerine had in spare, unemotional prose begun to tell an extraordinary story.

In November, he had led his special forces "A team"—ODA 574—into Afghanistan and helped local chieftains to organize an insurgency against the Taliban in the area north of Kandahar. When the Taliban learned what the Americans were up to, they immediately sent forces to enforce their own unique brand of justice and to slaughter every man, woman, and child in the village believed to be shielding the infidels. Captain Amerine and his soldiers had organized the village defenses and, aided by strong American air support, had routed a much larger force. The saga of that Alamo-like defense turned out to be the crux of a remarkable story. The accidental bombing, while tragic, was an unrelated incident that occurred more than two weeks later during what were essentially mopping-up operations.

Just before the press conference ended and we went back on-camera, I mouthed the word "Wow" at Rick Sanchez. He nodded and we found ourselves interviewing Captain Amerine and several of his soldiers. Rick always asked good questions in such circumstances and succeeded in highlighting the dramatic outlines of the story we had just heard. There really wasn't much for me to add, except for some "Gee whiz" questions about what this story said about Special Forces and how they were operating in this new kind of war. What I didn't trust myself to get into, however, were the emotions I was feeling. What had just played out on the TV screen, however, was a canonical example of what we tried to produce in a commander: someone who could accomplish challenging missions of great importance to the country, do so at a moment's notice, somehow succeed in spite of some very long odds; and having done all that, take care of his people to the absolute exclusion of himself. If I thought about it very much, there was the real danger of choking up in front of the cameras; since there was always the chance that the families of those Green Berets might be watching us on TV, that sort of thing would never, never do.

But I started thinking of Jason Amerine right then as the Anti-Enron, an iconic symbol of American military leadership when we finally got it right. At the very least, I figured that a more complete version of his story might even be worthwhile including in this book. It took more than three years, but the military is a small place and I eventually caught up with Jason Amerine, who coincidentally was teaching at West Point in the very same department that had nurtured Barry McCaffrey, Wayne Downing, Jack Jacobs, and me. It turned out that Jason was more of a maverick than he first seemed, a casualty of the manifold absurdities of the same Army officer evaluation system that had bedeviled me a generation earlier. The ethos of that system was summed up in the personnel officer's ancient adage, "I don't lie, but the truth might change." Apparently those people were still around, and Jason had run-ins that made it fortunate that he was even promoted to captain, and luckier yet to be selected for Special Forces.

He was commanding ODA 574—but still toying with resignation—when 9-11 struck. His team was brought back to the United States from a deployment to Kazakhstan with little question about their ultimate destination. By mid-October, he had said good-bye to his family and was placed in isolation—standard Special Forces practice before "going operational," but especially on an overseas combat assignment. While the Green Berets have a well-deserved image as ferocious fighters, their real function in war is the training of indigenous fighters as guerrillas. Jason's target was the Taliban, his assignment to link up with a warlord who had considerable stature in the area around Kandahar in southern Afghanistan. The warlord turned out to be Hamid Karzai, subsequently the first elected prime minister in Afghan's history. With the Taliban getting closer every day, Jason and his team took Karzai to a more secure location where, for two weeks, they put together a classic insurgency campaign plan.

Without a wealth of assets in the area, the Central Intelligence Agency (CIA) left him pretty much alone, although they were under intense pressure to get Special Forces teams operating on the ground. Karzai didn't believe it necessary to raise and train an entire army, reasoning that Jason's A-team might be enough to get the job done. Nevertheless they agreed to center their activities on the provincial capital of Tarin Kowt, where Karzai and the Americans infiltrated on the night of November 14, using the call sign "Texas 1-2." Afghan politics have not changed all that much since Rudyard Kipling's day and Tarin Kowt promptly hanged its Taliban-appointed mayor on November 15. Networking is as much a feature of tribal as well as advanced societies and by the sixteenth, word had spread that as many as a thousand Taliban were on their way to Tarin Kowt to wipe out the town in retribution.

Captain Amerine did what any good infantry officer would do in similar circumstances: he studied the terrain and quickly noticed a three-by-three mile constricted zone between the two mountain passes the Taliban would have to cross in order to attack the town. This was the key terrain, so Jason established his command post amidst a classic L-shaped ambush position on the second ridgeline overlooking Tarin Kowt. Although fighter aircraft were on call and lookouts were posted, the night of the sixteenth passed quietly. But at dawn on the morning of the seventeenth, just as if they were an Aggressor Battalion from the Army's National Training Center at Fort Irwin, California, a horde of Taliban appeared in pickup trucks, boiling through the pass and rushing into the open terrain beyond. Three F-18s, invisible above the morning fog, promptly attacked with laser-guided bombs. Ask any Texan, pickup trucks are fast-moving and elusive targets. Two bombs hit, one missed but the Taliban kept coming. Figuring that the opposing infidels must have some artillery, the Taliban were actually doing what a well-drilled attacking force should do—charging ahead even harder, just as the Mahdi cavalry had done when facing the British outside Omdurman more than a century earlier.

In those days, the British had lacked close air support, but as the Taliban broke out into the plain between the passes, Jason broadcast the prearranged emergency signal, "TROOPS IN CONTACT!" The three F-18s were now joined overhead by at least a dozen other aircraft and a hail of laser-guided bombs began to rain down on the Taliban vehicles. As more aircraft arrived, Jason divided his time between calling in air strikes and repositioning his own soldiers and trucks in the event of a breakthrough. Ground fire from the American ridgeline was beginning to strike the quickly closing Taliban forces, when the Navy's venerable F-14 fighter suddenly abandoned its usual Top Gun role for a final cameo appearance. The Green Berets remember it like a scene from a movie, the Tomcats dropping down through the clouds for unobstructed strafing runs against the profoundly shocked Taliban, who finally understood that they were not facing a band of surprisingly determined villagers but a lethal combination of American air and ground forces.

The attack quickly broke off but the punishment did not, the Taliban eventually leaving the field—now littered with as many as fifty burning trucks and three hundred dead or dying warriors.

Over the next two weeks, Karzai used the victory as political leverage to negotiate with both the Northern Alliance tribes and Taliban commanders, who were beginning to realize the game was up. Captain Amerine used the time to recruit and train more insurgents. Even Special Forces are not entirely insulated from adult supervision and, when his battalion commander arrived in early December, Jason tried to appear grateful for the help. The reinforced team, together with their new Afghan allies, was on a hilltop outside the village of Showalikot, when the battalion's recently arrived tactical air controller thought he might order up some air strikes against "holdouts" in some nearby positions. A B-52 with the snazzy new global positioning system (GPS)-guided joint direct attack munition (JDAM)—a ton of high explosives that could be steered to its target—was available; but the new controller committed a classic "rooky mistake" and entered his own coordinates into the guidance system. Jason remembers only the flash, the roar, and finding himself thrown to the ground some distance away. As many as fifty soldiers—most of them the new recruits—were killed, vaporized in an instant.

In a scene of unremitting horror and carnage, the survivors scrambled to sort themselves out, to care for the wounded and dying, and remembering the basics, to secure their own position against a possible counterattack. Jason was among the hundred wounded, hit by shrapnel and losing both ear drums, but far worse was finding two members of his team who had been killed instantly: Sgt.1c Dan Petithory and the team's top noncommissioned officer (NCO), M. Sgt. Jefferson Davis, or "J.D." It took four hours for the team to be medevaced out through Amman, Jordan, arriving in Landstuhl on December 7. Jason stayed a day later, escorting the team's dead and arriving in Landstuhl just before the press conference began on the 8th. Along the way, he had plenty of time to think, recalling a dark incident from early in his career when a news blackout had prevented several members of his unit from getting the official recognition he felt they deserved. But not this time. When asked by the Landstuhl medical authorities if he would be willing to address their press conference, he coolly replied, "Yes, I will do the press conference as long as I get to say what these men did." The method to his madness was that by publicizing what ODA 574 had accomplished in combat, rather than celebrating their victimhood, there was a far better chance that soldiers like J.D. and Dan would get the recognition due them, albeit posthumously.

And in the end that is exactly the way it worked out: Silver Stars were awarded to Master Sergeant Davis and Sergeant First Class Petithory for gallantry in combat against an armed enemy of the United States—certainly an apt description of both them and the Taliban. Captain Amerine is now Major Amerine and a West Point faculty assignment can be a well-recognized pathway to a star; even so, one simply does not ask if "the system" exacted any retribution against Jason for going public in the way he had. I intended to conclude our interview by simply asking, "Was it worth it?" and Jason replied quickly that it certainly had been. But he then astonished me by adding that his father also agreed completely with that assessment because he had seen our interview on MSNBC as it was occurring.

It is not often that one gets to speak directly with one of our audience members, but this was not an opportunity to be missed. Ronald Amerine, a retired educator now living in Hawaii, is deeply proud of his son, not only for what he did in Afghanistan but also for keeping faith with his fellow soldiers. He also vividly remembers the interview between Jason, Rick Sanchez, and me. It came only hours after receiving the grimly worded telegram about his son having been wounded in combat and was the first time he had seen him since sending him off to war three months earlier. Jason's sudden appearance on network television was a substantial relief as well as a thrill "that took away some of the dark" from the life of an anxious parent. It turned out that part of the reason the elder Amerine was watching MSNBC was because our coverage regularly featured military analysts like Barry McCaffrey and Jack Jacobs. We seemed almost like kin, knowing what we could and couldn't say, while instinctively appreciating sacrifice and heroism. Barry and Jack, of course, had long since earned the medals to prove their own heroism, while I had simply been lucky enough and adopted long enough to recognize that this sort of thing ran in the family. You have now learned enough about him to make up your own mind; but regardless of whether the Army is eventually smart enough to pin stars on his shoulders, Jason Amerine symbolizes all that we really mean when we describe ourselves as soldiers—first, last, and always.

---

[1] Portions of the following paragraphs are drawn from the account previously published in my book, *Business as War*, (New York: Wiley, 2004), 5, 12.

[2] For a fuller account of Major Leibner's heroism, see David M. Shribman, "One Year after Plunging into the Fire," *Boston Globe*, September 8, 2002.

[3] See Jim Rutenberg, "At Fox News, The Colonel Who Wasn't," *New York Times*, April 29, 2002.

The author (right) with Jed Babbin, also an author and television "talking head," in Al Rustimayah, Iraq, December 2005. Babbin coined the term "Warheads" to show that former warriors in front of the camera were a new kind of media animal. *Author's collection*

The commentator's perspective: CNN's Don Shepperd on the set in Washington. *Courtesy CNN*

The CNN control room, Washington. *Courtesy CNN*

The generals of Bosnia (l. to r.): Wesley Clark, Eric Shinseki, and David Grange. Bosnia would prove to be a crossroads for the future "Warheads," as three of them—Grange, Clark, and the author—served there. *Courtesy David Grange*

The generals of CNN (l. to r.): Don Shepperd, Wesley Clark, and David Grange, having made the transition from warrior to Warhead. *Courtesy CNN*

Retired Major General Bob Scales (right), now an analyst for Fox News, during a recent trip to Iraq. *Courtesy Bob Scales*

Warhead Bill Cowan (left) with Tony Snow, then affiliated with Fox News, now Presidential spokesman. *Courtesy Bill Cowan*

The boys of MSNBC: The author (left) and Jack Jacobs on duty. *Courtesy MSNBC*

Rick Francona on MSNBC. *Courtesy MSNBC*

Fox analyst Tom McInerny with Lieutenant Nicole Barnum, USAF, in Baghdad.
Author's collection

Retired Air Force Lieutenant Commander
Jim Clapper, who transformed the National
Geospatial Intelligence Agency into a
warfighting tool during the War on Terror.
NGI official photo

Lieutenant General Dave Petraeus (left) pictured here with Lieutenant General Abdul Qadr, chief of the Iraqi ground forces. Petraeus was given "mission impossible": training a competent Iraqi security force from the ground up after a critical year had been lost. *U.S. Army photo*

Afghanistan, 2003: Captain Jason Amerine (white brimmed hat, right of center) and the members of Special Forces A-team with future Afghan Prime Minister Hamid Karzai (dark turban, center). *Courtesy Jason Amerine*

They call it "irregular warfare" for a reason. Jasone Amerine (back of truckbed, right) in a modern chariot in Tarin Kowt two weeks after the battle. Seated alongside Amerine is "Allan," the team's Air Force combat controller. *Courtesy Jason Amerine*

Jason Amerine (left) with Hamid Karzai, Kabul, 2003. *Courtesy Jason Amerine*

CHAPTER FIVE

The Warheads and the Secretary

· · · · ·

The war in Afghanistan was over almost before it began. By December 22, Hamid Karzai had been sworn in as the interim head of the post-Taliban government. Any way you looked at it, this was a significant triumph of American arms. The Russian army, crown jewel one of the world's toughest and most ruthless military machines, had been bled white in the Afghan snows and mountain passes for a decade before a withdrawal that foreshadowed the collapse of the Soviet state. The Russians, of course, had been much closer to the neighborhood, which made the triumph even more satisfying because American forces had endured an eight-thousand-mile trek just to arrive on the scene. The combined arms partnership displayed to such good effect at Tarin Kowt—Special Forces on the ground and American air power at all points above it—proved devastating. In one of the key battles outside Marzar-i-Sharif, for example, American Green Berets on horseback had again worked in close coordination with B-52 pilots to show what properly employed JDAMs could really accomplish. Rolling barrages of the one-ton weapons—pinpointed to ten-meter accuracy—had obliterated Taliban defenses, scattered the survivors, and admirably clarified the remaining issues for those thinking about switching their loyalties.

It was the latest wrinkle in the age-old yin-and-yang relationship between the soldier and the scientist. Students in my Georgetown classes had been asked to trace this relationship all the way back to the Greeks and the Romans, always alert for the perpetual issue of trade-offs between armor, weight, and mobility, or fortification versus penetrating weapons. As important: the never-ending rivalry between those seeking an advantage in combat by harnessing the fruits of technology and those persistently ferocious little gnomes down through history who live for the exquisite pleasure of overturning any such advantage. In the twentieth century, technology provided spectacular opportunities for new applications of these old arguments, never more so than in the unending debates over the role of airpower, debates that had not been entirely settled by the advent of strategic bombing in World War II or even the emergence of the U.S. Air Force as a coequal military service in 1947. The Cold War was barely over when the arguments were started all over again by marriage of stealth aircraft, precision munitions, and vast improvements in the whole panoply of intelligence and targeting technologies.[1]

Some of the more profound ideas in the current round could be traced back to one of our occasional Warhead colleagues, Col. John Warden, a former Air Force officer and dean of the Air War College. Those were ample credentials by themselves, but in 1988 Warden had written a book that redefined our whole notion of what an air campaign was supposed to achieve. Just two years later, those ideas became the blueprint for the aerial assault on Baghdad that opened a whole new chapter in military history. "War can be won from the air," Warden had confidently declared at the time and his words seemed prophetic.[2] Rarely does a single technology spark a revolution, but when the quantum leaps in computers and digital communications were added to everything else, the Air Force was finally beginning to approach the Elysian heights long envisioned by classical airpower theory. It was called the "revolution in military affairs," or RMA, and while the Air Force held no monopoly on its applications, determinists in light blue uniforms could often be found leading the chants before the altar of technology.

Afghanistan had merely been the latest demonstration that Murphy's Law had not entirely been dispelled by these incantations. The problem was that the pilot flying over the battlefield in a stealth aircraft was merely the human element of an "extended weapon system" stretching thousands of miles back to "the wizards at Langley" (the self-descriptive term for the CIA Technical Operations Directorate).[3] Lots of things could go wrong along the way, whether the "delivery system" was a bomber or a cruise missile. Often it seemed as if we had become far better at hitting things than knowing just what those things really were, as in Khartoum when we hit a chemical weapons laboratory that turned out to be a laxative factory. During the war over Kosovo, we hit the Chinese Embassy in Belgrade that turned out to be...well...the Chinese Embassy. Bad as that seemed at the time, there was a happy outcome, despite days of violent anti-American demonstrations in Peking. The more we apologized and geekily explained that the unfortunate incident was due to a mapping error or some digital anomaly, the more convinced the Chinese became that we couldn't possibly be *that* stupid, that we must know they were up to something and they should damned well behave themselves before the U.S. military became *really* angry. So all's well that ends well, but having the extended weapon system gave one a certain empathy for the Will Smith character in the movie *I, Robot*.

Such glitches aside, the technology had a further side-effect: it produced great videos. The appetite for such footage had become insatiable beginning with the first Persian Gulf War, with its images of cruise missiles flying down the streets of Baghdad. Ever since, each new American engagement regularly featured compelling videos of missiles hitting buildings, bridges, and (occasionally) people with pinpoint accuracy. Both sides of the conflict had been caught up in the wonderful new game. Throughout the 1990s, the Air Force regularly patrolled the "no-fly zone" imposed on Iraq after the first Gulf War; the patrols had become a deadly contest between American pilots and Iraqi air defenders. When air defense targets were attacked or other sites bombed in reprisal for Saddam's violations of the cease-fire accords, his regime was always eager to demonstrate American aggression and high handedness. Accordingly remote TV cameras had been more or less permanently installed close to the obvious downtown targets. Although it was an odd arrangement, in reality everybody won: the mainstream networks got higher ratings, the Iraqis got grist for the mills of Al Jazeera, while the Pentagon got stirring pictures that might later be useful in winning public support for its war policies.

This was the practical side of "information operations," the understanding that information had become so fundamental to warfare that to neglect it like a toddler left unattended beside a busy highway was to guarantee that disaster had also not been left to chance. Instead what the Soviets had once called "active measures" were called for, not just to "spin" a story but to shape the larger environment where the whole yarn would be received, believed, and acted upon. The problem was that once you started down that road, the information spectrum was so vast that there was no practical way of knowing where and when to stop. New terms were needed and constantly supplied: information dominance, information assurance, information-age warfare, and more to the point, information warfare.[4]

Eventually, these terms and even the whole concept of the RMA became entirely subsumed into the ambitious Transformation Agenda Donald Rumsfeld staked out when he took the reins at the Pentagon. His motto seemed to be "faster, lighter, and more efficient through the fielding of ever-higher technology." Through much of his early tenure, working groups were constantly empanelled, with white papers drafted and re-drafted. Machiavelli is supposed to have written that if you want to see people at their worst, just try changing the order of things; so when they realized Rumsfeld was really serious, opponents dug in their heels. My phone conversation with Jim Miklaszewski the day before 9-11 was not only a routine exchange of post-Labor Day pleasantries but also included some speculation about how long "Rummie" could last, since he seemed indifferent to the influential constituencies he was alienating. Whatever else changed within the next twenty-four hours, the secretary of defense had been seemingly vindicated and Transformation established as the principal road ahead. Ret. Vice Adm. Arthur Cebrowski was brought in to head the effort and, in congressional testimony the following spring, he left little doubt about the scope of the required changes:

> First, and foremost, military transformation is about culture. Revolutionary capabilities do not come solely from technology. Transformation must institutionalize a culture of change and innovation in order to maintain a competitive advantage in the information age. That culture must foster leadership, education, processes, organizations, values, attitudes and beliefs that encourage and reward meaningful innovation.[5]

Both transformation and information operations presupposed an activist approach to the news, but throughout much of 2002, the Warheads' TV time was dominated by three rather straightforward stories: the aftermath of the war in Afghanistan—often synonymous with the hunt for Osama bin Laden and escaped Taliban leaders; the movement of captured Al Qaida fighters to the new detention facility at Guantánamo; and the steady buildup of U.S. forces and logistics around the Persian Gulf region. The need to cover those stories meant that all the cable networks were consistently using their military analysts, if less frantically than during the days immediately following 9-11. It wasn't clear if the country was settling in for the long haul in the war on terror or just turning away. Months before, I had been signed by Leading Authorities, a Washington-based speakers bureau, that suddenly found itself booking me for lecture dates all over the country. In May 2002, I gave a speech to a business audience meeting at a resort in Arizona—usually an enthusiastic crowd, but not this time; while cordial, they seemed…a little distracted. Later during the reception, I asked the sponsor about it. No, no, no, he said, it had been a fine speech. It was just that these folks were from the west coast and their real estate development businesses had never been better. The war seemed like an east coast thing and the only time they even thought much about it was when they might have the bad luck to get frisked before boarding a plane.

So soon after 9-11, this was a startling insight, prompting distant memories not only of Yossi's Gap but also of more recent ones, notably my oft-repeated, ludicrously incautious, highly public, and clearly wrong assertions that now, after the American homeland had been attacked, the United States would surely mobilize its population and declare war. It didn't happen, of course. Instead, President Bush had apparently felt it more essential to rebuild American confidence and self-esteem. So rather than asking the able-bodied to enlist for the armed services, they were instead urged to join in a lemming-like return to the malls, or even better, to emplane for shopping expeditions elsewhere in the country, although, of course, at the considerable risk of being frisked. So Americans had returned to their shopping habits, reboarded their airplanes and continued to outsource their military service requirements to other peoples' kids, which was OK as long as you were fighting a war like Afghanistan. That adventure had clearly been a come-as-you-are party in which the top echelons of the military-professional food chain—Special Forces and fighter-bomber pilots—had prevailed over hordes of Taliban fanatics.

What was not clear was how long this stance on the manpower issue could be maintained if we either got into a large-scale war in Iraq or if the war on terror stretched out to the generational horizons that some analysts were suggesting. The reason was pretty simple, although few Americans were even remotely famil-iar with it. As the Cold War ended and the military was reduced, or "downsized," the remaining forces were organized around a smaller active force, backed by a reserve component that could quickly be recalled to service in a crisis or similar emergency. However, it had always been assumed that any more protracted situ-ation, such as a garden-variety conventional war, would require some form of national service to fill the ranks. The reserves, then, were simply meant to fill the gap until those manpower needs could be met—that is, the nation's manpower called to the colors and then organized, trained, equipped, and sent off to war in the manner of previous generations.[6] Except that as 2002 wore on and the con-flict with Iraq drew nearer, the only thing that was happening was that reserve forces were being called up every day; indeed the active force depended so heav-ily upon its supposedly part-time components that there was virtually no way one could be "tasked" without involving the other. Yet no other manpower was being called into existence to fill the gaps as the reserves were called up. Even as the active force prepared for war, it was not being expanded nor was anything beyond the usual enlistments even being contemplated.

It sometimes seemed as if the Warheads had once again been drafted, this time as translator-substitutes providing the military literacy bred out of ordinary Americans by the end of conscription a generation earlier. We were regularly in and out of the studios of all three cable networks, appearing in morning shows, individual hits during day-side programming, and panel shows during prime time. Increasingly, too, the themes of all that programming began to turn more toward Iraq. At the same time, it was difficult not to notice Rumsfeld, who had by now become a hyperactive TV performer in his own right, constantly in front of the cameras for weekly thrust-and-parry sessions with the Pentagon press corps, photo ops, and almost every other conceivable occasion. As his press secretary later noted, "By the spring of 2002, Rumsfeld had already conducted more briefings, interviews and outreach meetings than three of his predecessors put together."[7] What we had no way of knowing at the time was that the people around Rumsfeld, like Torie Clarke, were also pretty good observers of who else besides their boss was routinely on television. And right now it was us.

During the Clinton years, we had routinely joked that our on-air comments during Kosovo and the various dustups with Iraq must have placed us so high up on a White House enemies' list that we would be fortunate to be admitted to the Easter Monday Egg Roll on the South Lawn. The reality was that the Clinton people had studiously ignored us, despite the growth of cable TV and its annoying habit of reacting to any international crisis by calling upon the growing stable of Warheads for what was often some very pointed commentary. It may have been part of their larger "information operations" strategy, but the Rumsfeld Pentagon would not make that same mistake, especially if war with Iraq was on the way. Part of the same strategy, but far from the public eye or our studio cameras, was that the secretary of defense was beginning the first moves in an outreach campaign that would embrace the military analysts then shooting off our mouths on TV. While it was meant to bring us inside the fold, the thing about information operations is that their outcomes are often unpredictable. In an odd way, by bringing us together for his own purposes, Rumsfeld would also create the Warheads as a self-aware band of brothers.

In the fall of 2002 a series of discreet phone calls to my office established my tentative willingness to come into the Pentagon for briefings organized by the secretary of defense, calls which were quickly compared with close friends like Barry McCaffrey and Jed Babbin. "Last thing we need these days is to be bore-assed to death by high-ranking action officers clicking off PowerPoints" was a typical response. Several days later, however, a follow-up phone call set the hook: the secretary of defense would be present for at least some of the briefings, and would I kindly consent to be his guest? One had to admire the brilliance of the move: the benign neglect of the Clintonistas would now be replaced by tête-à-têtes with the Mighty, even the Almighty Himself if Rumsfeld really showed up. I reported it all up the NBC chain of command, Miklaszewski losing no time in teasing me about being called in for the "secret handshake" while he and his colleagues in the regular Pentagon press corps were struggling every day to eat or be eaten. However, the ground rules specified that most of the briefings were "on background," meaning that anything said publicly could be attributed only to "senior defense officials." It was also clear going in that it was unlikely we would be told anything that might have led one of our anchors to look into the cameras and say, "We are now going to break away from our minute-by-minute coverage of today's fiery collision of three tractor trailers on the New Jersey Turnpike in order to bring you *this* late-breaking bulletin from our MSNBC military analyst...."

No, what was going on here was all about nuance, subtlety, and access. While on active duty, all the military analysts had held security clearances, often with "special access" that went well beyond top secret. Some of those clearances were still in effect, the result of various board memberships, part-time consulting contracts, or full-time jobs, usually not far removed from the defense establishment where we had spent so many years. We were granted a privileged, "insider" view because, the theory seemed to be, we knew or could guess much of what was going on, so we could also be trusted not to say too much. Nor was there any question that the extraordinary level of access was itself a part of the privilege. Since 9-11, it had become considerably easier to cross most borders than to gain access to the Pentagon, where security was now an impenetrable barrier. Many repairs to the building were completed within a year and in the new visitors center even a retired military ID card granted no exemption from sequential searches by machine-gun-toting guards. The difference now was that we were guests of the secretary: we went from frisk to whisk, escorted through security and past the envious stares of the unwashed by respectful young soldiers detailed from the Honor Guard and wearing full dress uniforms.

Once at the secretary's conference room, our cell phones were checked at the door and we entered the inner sanctum. The room was well appointed though hardly ostentatious by Washington standards; but with carpets, recessed lighting, and china coffee cups, clearly at the top end of the government food chain. The room was dominated by a long, narrow wooden conference table around which the Warheads gathered, our places assigned by neatly lettered place cards with the highest ranks closest to the top. My usual vantage point—at the opposite end—had a certain plebeian charm, but the most enjoyable part of the meeting was the chance to mingle freely with friends and colleagues of long standing. Gen. Barry McCaffrey was there, a division commander in the first Gulf War and now a frequent interlocutor on NBC and MSNBC. Both of us had taught at West Point, so it was natural to fall in with Lt. Gen. Dan Christman, the recently retired Military Academy superintendent who was now starting as an analyst with CNN. Once there, Dan had joined forces with Maj. Gen. Dave Grange, Air Force Lt. Gen. Don Shepperd, as well as with another prominent West Point alum, Gen. Wes Clark. I had known Wes for twenty years; now he was fast gaining notoriety for his articulate public policy positions—not always related to defense—both on TV and in front of political groups across the country. The Fox News contingent usually included Lt. Gen. Tom McInerny, Maj. Gen. Paul Vallely, Maj. Gen. Bob Scales, and Lt. Col. Bill Cowan.

It was a fun group. Most of us had come to know one another at various points in our military careers; but with our media affiliations we now had new war stories to share with one another and the quips came fast and furious. Whenever he could, Lt. Gen. Bernard Trainor joined us from Boston. A retired Marine, Mick Trainor was a gifted storyteller who had also been the military correspondent of the *New York Times* and a professor at Harvard's Kennedy School of Government.[8] Great titles all; however, among us he was known as "Eminence," the accolade earned when he reported in haste for an MSNBC hit in our Boston studios and only had time to don a camel-hair blazer over a red turtle-neck sweater. Thereafter he became known informally as Bernard Cardinal Trainor of Boston, all of us agreeing that had Mick chosen a career in the Church over his beloved Corps, the archdiocese of Boston would have found that it had much better discipline and a lot fewer problems.

The run-up to the meeting also provided a chance to compare notes with each other about our new media careers. Maj. Gen. Dave Grange had joined CNN just after 9-11 and not long after leaving command of the Army's famed Big Red One (1st Infantry Division). However, the last time I had seen him was during the war in Kosovo in 1999 when three of his troops had been captured by a Serb special operations unit, spirited back across the border and then held as POWs before Jesse Jackson flew in and engineered their release. Throughout that crisis, Dave had been on TV every day. What was not widely known was that he had held several key positions on the Army staff in the mid-'90s as the service tried to come to grips with the new concept of information operations and, typical for the Army, to place it in a sensible context of doctrine.

Had any of that background helped when he suddenly found himself on the air every day? "It sure did," he replied. "With information operations, the power is there: the only question is if you use it or lose it." By building up his division's capabilities in the new discipline, Dave had also engineered close working relationships with several reporters, including Jon Anderson of *Stars & Stripes*. When his soldiers first turned up missing, Dave had persuaded Anderson to sit on the story for six hours until search and rescue operations could confirm the abduction; shortly thereafter the *Stars & Stripes* exclusive made headlines around the world. "Seems fair enough," I replied. "But did anybody complain about compromising the public's right to know?" "Nope, not at all," said Dave. "We eventually got those kids back. But their families heard the bad news from us first, not from some garbled news report." At that point, both of us looked around the conference room at our colleagues and broke into rueful smiles. Like Pogo we had now met the enemy, and he was us.

Put two or more of the Warheads in a room together for any length of time and the laughter and noise levels were sure to rise. But not matter how engrossing our side conversations, all the grab ass ended abruptly when Donald Rumsfeld walked into the room, because he dominated any gathering, any space, any conversation, and any group of lesser mortals, which clearly included all of us. Here was a man who was on TV more than we were, dressed better than we did, and had a "command presence" any general could only envy. Then writing a business book, I was well attuned to Rumsfeld's corporate background and the usual characterizations of him as a "quintessential CEO." Maybe, but he always reminded me more of Harry Truman, a cocky, bantam rooster of a man who could casually take your head off in an argument, and grin at you the whole time.

Only once in all our times together did I try to challenge him: when he later decreed that the commanders-in-chief of the field combatant commands (the CINCs or SINKS) would henceforth simply be called "commanders." Under our Constitution, only the president deserved the title of commander-in-chief, Rumsfeld reasoned, not the generals. But as an Army congressional aide, I had worked on that 1986 legislation which reformed the structure of those commands and was almost certain that Congress had purposely used the title of CINCs in describing those positions. At our next meeting I asked him about it: off the top of his head, he quoted me chapter and verse to show that his interpretation, not my recollection, was correct. And then flashed that famous grin, the same way that a defensive back extends a helping hand to the wide receiver he's just flattened.

It was difficult not to like and admire him, to enjoy our meetings or his frequent jousts with the Pentagon press corps. In her memoir, Press Secretary Torie Clarke records one typical encounter:

> One…reporter…made the mistake of strongly insinuating the answer—the wrong answer—in a question posed to Rumsfeld. The secretary paused, peered down at the reporter and laced him. "First of all, you're beginning with an illogical premise and proceeding perfectly logically to an illogical conclusion…which is a dangerous thing to do."[9]

MSNBC took to covering at least a portion of his press references live because they usually provided at least a few headlines as well as some fireworks. Time and again, we would hear Rumsfeld pause and then start winding up for his backhand with a characteristic phrase like "Well, my goodness…" and you just knew that the ball was coming back across the net toward a hapless reporter far faster than it had arrived. On his primetime show Keith Olberman took to parodying "The Poetry of Donald Rumsfeld" by isolating fragments of his best-known sayings like, "There are the known knowns and the known unknowns. And then there are the unknown unknowns."

Torie Clarke makes a point of noting that part of the Pentagon's communications strategy in those years was an insistence on acknowledging and quickly getting on top of bad news, a sensible recognition that neither dead fish nor bad news improve very much with age. Except that pinning Rumsfeld down on a mistake or anything else where he did not wish to be pinned down was a feat in itself. It was the Nixon White House that invented the exquisitely neutral phrase, "mistakes were made," to word-smith and otherwise camouflage their most egregious shenanigans. Often the same dynamic appeared to operate with Rumsfeld, because intelligence findings were never "wrong" nor were strategic plans, logistical estimates, or battlefield outcomes either SNAFU or even FUBAR. Instead he might—and only on rare occasions—concede that some of these things could have been "imperfect."

He was a consummate forensic artist, always "on message" and never flustered. During one of our Warhead meetings a briefer confided to us that "while I don't want to get too far out in front of the secretary," it was pretty common knowledge Rumsfeld wished to reduce U.S. troop commitments to a particular Asian nation— call it South Neuralgia. An hour later, Rumsfeld himself was in front of us taking questions on U.S. troop deployments and arguing that no firm decisions on those reductions had yet been made. Protecting the source, one of our number smoothly asked him, "But, sir, we hear that you really want to reduce American troop levels in South Neuralgia." Rumsfeld never missed a beat, "Oh *really*?" he replied innocently. The room exploded into laughter, and to his credit, Rumsfeld joined in. Such scenes inevitably prompted a recurrent thought: that if you were invited to one of those interminable Washington dinner parties, almost any subterfuge could be justified if it succeeded in getting you a seat at Donald Rumsfeld's table.

But the problem was this: striking as these characteristics were, they did not always endear Donald Rumsfeld to the professional military or to others in positions of power around Washington. Everyone recognized Rumsfeld's characteristic impatience with fools and some suspected that this was precisely the box into which his carefully ordered mind had placed them. Even before we became enmeshed in Iraq, it was no mystery why some people compared him to Robert McNamara. I'd had passing acquaintances with seven different defense secretaries over the years, and there was no question that Rumsfeld (the only person to have ever held that job twice) was by far the most formidable public servant I had ever encountered. On the other hand, I didn't have to work for him every day either. He commanded great loyalty from many of his closest advisers, who tended to stress how devoted he was to building consensus in the decision process; but from the earliest days of his tenure, Rumsfeld had also been a lightning rod for dissension and disagreement, which could frequently take on a disagreeably personal tone. His impatience with the generals and the Pentagon bureaucracy was already legendary, but up to a point, that was admirable too. Generals and bureaucrats frequently need to be shaken up because they have a way of wandering into ruts—distinguishable from graves only because the ends have been knocked out. But especially in war the trick for any civilian political leader is to know when to override the judgment of his military chiefs and when to defer, trusting that their knowledge of this grim craft is superior to his own.

Striking that critical balance has been a recurring theme in military history: what Clausewitz called the "culminating point of victory" was also familiar to World War II historian Cornelius Ryan as "A Bridge Too Far." In late 2002 the timely arrival of a book recently published by my friend, Eliot Cohen, drew my attention. Eliot had been a fellow student at Harvard, mentored by Samuel Huntington and now developing his own formidable reputation as a strategic thinker. His book—a surprisingly easy read for a volume on civil-military relations—had compared the styles of four great wartime leaders: Abraham Lincoln, Georges Clemenceau, Winston Churchill, and David Ben-Gurion. Each could be irascible, infuriating, and notably disinclined to accept the traditional boundaries separating the soldier from the politician; yet they rarely were autocratic and often even promoted those who had disagreed with them most strongly. This was, of course, hard going for the generals "who found themselves broken down by the strain of managing a war while in turn being managed by a civilian leader who treated military advice as [nothing more than] that."[10] Despite the trouble it took to conduct this inherently "unequal dialogue," it was critical for the elected official's ability to function in a situation where everyone might be more or less wrong and the challenge was to discern "when others are even more wrong than oneself." Precisely because the military view is a partial and probably conventional one, the political master must be ever alert to the new truths that define a situation: "the statesman's art of perception lies in *seeing*, embedded in a mass of detail, that which is indeed new and different."[11]

Instead of micro-management, the politician's art meant looking tirelessly for nuances, subtleties, new patterns, or anything else that might challenge standing assumptions no matter how devoutly cherished. That was a tall order for any leader in business, war, or politics, but Eliot had a point, especially since the novel features of the new global war on terror seemed to have swept away the more traditional features of the defense landscape. However, his book had to be read in snatches because when not preparing to help MSNBC cover the Iraq war, I was writing my own book on business leadership.[12] In the aftermath of the Enron meltdown, even the term "business leadership" seemed out of place. Congress was huffily working on ever-more impenetrable and intrusive compliance standards, ensuring full employment for unborn generations of regulators, auditors, and accountants. Caught up in the spirit of the thing, one of my speeches may also have gone somewhat over the top when I rudely joked that corporate executives tended to be "overpaid hacks with tiny little dicks." No matter, the serious concern was that the American corporate leadership culture, which had produced Donald Rumsfeld, was hardly the kind of place that encouraged subtlety and a Zen-like sensitivity for nuance.

The former CEO of G.D. Searle & Company, Rumsfeld was by that point still being lionized as a "battle-hardened maverick" whose leadership lessons suggested "the Pentagon's answer to Harry Truman."[13] (Apparently my comments were not the only ones that had gone over the top.) But from my reading of American business leadership, there seemed to be four reasons for concern as Donald Rumsfeld prepared to become the principal leader of the Iraq war effort.

1. Donald Rumsfeld was the quintessential rationalist and technologist, bringing his well-known penchant for organization to every task—just as a proper CEO should. Hardworking and industrious, he customarily toiled while standing at an elevated desk in his office, endlessly questioning the assumptions of the bureaucracy. All these were precisely the characteristics you would of course want in a Pentagon chief, but there was also that theological faith in the scientific method and its technological applications. Those tendencies had been reinforced by his background as a naval aviator, which was hardly a disqualification in itself, but the Navy tended to look at things from an operational-strategic perspective. Its maps were typically 1:250,000 or higher: Iraq was going to be a war in the weeds where victory would be a function of tactics carried out by commanders with 1:50,000 maps and scribbled-in grid coordinates. Rumsfeld had all the right credentials as a data-driven, hard-charging executive, but this struggle, as Cohen had suggested, might take more of an artist.

2. The Enron scandal underlined one of the defining traits of modern American corporate culture: the isolation of its top leaders. Physical as well as psychological, this isolation can become a cocoon of wishful thinking surrounding the CEO, reinforced by his staff, their procedures, and even by the typical confines of the executive suite. While there are a number of excellent books

written on the topic (although I concede a certain fondness for my own) the most reliable guide is this: simply poll the rank and file at most Fortune 500 companies and go with their verdict. This was precisely the culture that had produced Donald Rumsfeld, rewarded him handsomely, and even elevated him to near-iconic status.

While the military is an institution that knows all about rank and its privileges, the top-down management style of the corporate world is tempered in the world of the warrior by the give-and-take recognition of both shared danger and the teamwork required to succeed in any operation. But because survival skills are well honed, any military unit quickly learns to appreciate what the new boss does not want to hear, what they may not say without incurring some degree of risk, and what they may not ask him without appearing to be the dumbest guys on the planet. With his iron-jawed determination and unbeatable forensic skills, there was every opportunity for subordinate military commanders to interpret Donald Rumsfeld's supreme self-confidence as arrogance, to sit on inconvenient information, or worst of all, to "dumb down" or otherwise filter out questions that might seem unwelcome. An essential skill for the CEO, this could hardly be the best thing if you were scouting for nuance or the defining detail in a war of uncertain dimensions.

3. It was a point closely related to the business about figuring out what the boss really did not want to hear; but for all their obsession with information, corporate executives often seemed curiously indifferent to intelligence. Usually they ignored it, substituted less rigorous "market research," or simply believed what they wanted to believe. Rumsfeld was surely the exception: not only the current but a former secretary of defense, a member of numerous boards and commissions, and an executive well known for understanding the value of accurate intelligence.[14] However, I had once worked for another prominent executive who had come to the Pentagon not really understanding that great efforts were required just to seek out the bad news, let alone deal with it once it arrived. A fine man, he later seemed surprised when the bureaucracy ate him. Like most conventional business executives, he understood little about intelligence and even less about counterintelligence: the need to turn that telescope inward to discover the bad news before it got even worse or to pick up on those all-important nuances. Ironically the secretary requesting his resignation had been Dick Cheney, and whatever had become of him? Surely Rumsfeld would not make that same mistake?

4. One of the monographs regularly assigned to my Georgetown classes was a RAND paper focusing on the major differences distinguishing four of the

most enduring organizational patterns throughout history; two of which were hierarchies and networks. From primitive tribes all the way up to CNN, networks had been built around the smooth transfer of information while hierarchies were all about the seamless exchange of orders and accountability.[15] Now two of the most advanced examples of those structures, the Pentagon and Al Qaida, were locked in a war to the death. All warfare is about adaptation, but even after 9-11 it was an open question if anyone could get the Pentagon—famously and even notoriously resistant to change—to make the necessary modifications in time to make a difference. Donald Rumsfeld certainly appeared to have the required leadership skills, yet he was even more the product of an embedded hierarchy than most of the people who worked in the Pentagon.

It was one thing to talk about the need for transformation—many had done that, many times before—but how would he adapt the centralized, rules-based department he now ran to challenge the agile decentralized networks of the terrorists, essentially malevolent tribes with bad attitudes and cell phones? If nuance was essential to the task, so too was a close reading of history—the very reason why those overworked Georgetown students were made to study the Greek phalanx and the Roman legion. The key questions were always about how well any military structure had adapted to the demands of its physical or political environments, and technology was never the sole answer. In fact, the only certainty was uncertainty because war with a smart, tenacious, and rather vicious adversary had a way of producing some unexpected waypoints.

Important as they may have been, these issues seemed like distant thunder as the buildup against Iraq continued steadily into the winter months of 2002–3. The Warhead briefings continued as well with an interesting new wrinkle. While the meetings had started out as gatherings of the media analysts, they now routinely seemed to include prominent people who seldom appeared on the air, retired generals, members of the Council on Foreign Relations, and senior fellows of various Washington think tanks. Everyone, including us, seemed to be trading on some form of access to the powerful—long established in the nation's capital as its second oldest industry—but no one seemed concerned about any possible conflicts of interest. NBC and MSNBC encouraged us to attend whenever possible. The organizers of the briefings had tactfully dropped our original moniker as "Retired Military Advisers to the Secretary of Defense" but the whole thing reminded me of an old academic jibe about drunks and lampposts: that we were being used more for support than illumination.

Advisers or not, the decisions Rumsfeld now faced over Iraq were twofold: not only the familiar one of "How far is too far?" but also "What kind of a force will be required to accomplish the mission?" Throughout the transformation debates, the ground forces had always seemed hopelessly retro; when those issues came up during his conversations with the Warheads, the secretary often talked about the high costs of manpower investments and the backwardness of Army force structure. Ideas have consequences; while the exact order of battle remained highly classified, our Pentagon briefings suggested that the assault on Baghdad might be entrusted to no more than four Army and Marine Corps divisions. Despite having to cross three hundred miles of desert into the heart of Iraq to destroy its enemies, the American ground force now arrayed on the Iraqi border was less than half the size of the one sent a decade earlier to fight in Operation Desert Storm. Only one of the Warheads knew the full extent of the behind-the-scenes conflict that was occurring at precisely this moment. General Trainor would later write,

> Rumsfeld and his commanders looked at troop requests through opposite ends of the telescope. The defense secretary approached these requisitions with the ruthless efficiency of a businessman for whom excess inventory was to be avoided at all costs....Rumsfeld regularly told Pentagon officials that the United States had sent more forces and supplies (during Desert Storm) than were needed and the Iraqi military was weaker than it had been in 1991. For Rumsfeld, too large a buildup was not only a waste of effort and a violation of the new way to wage war but a drag on the deployment phase.[16]

This civil-military divergence affected the size and composition of the force as well as the order in which these units were to be deployed. Rumsfeld regarded as a "wasteful anachronism" the computerized time-phased force deployment list (TPFDL) on which the military had relied for a generation to regulate the orderly flow of troops and equipment to the war zone. The result, as one general later recalled: "Because they didn't use a TPFDL, I think we were inefficient in flowing forces over there....There was reluctance to mobilize reserve components prior to Christmas" despite the fact that the Reserves were fundamental logistical building blocks to everything else. The resulting turbulence would create waves that would wash up in unlikely places, eventually even being linked to the Abu Ghraib prison scandal and the uncoordinated deployment of reservists comprising military police units at the prison.[17]

All of our networks had kept the Warheads informed of many of these conflicts because, even with military secrecy, such disputes were hard to keep under wraps. The Chairman of the Joint Chiefs of Staff, Gen. Richard Myers, the nation's top-ranking military officer, had even appeared at one of our briefings to stress that the campaign plan was a good one and that it had been thoroughly vetted and agreed to by the Joint Chiefs—the institution legally charged with providing military advice to the nation's political leaders. While there was no "party line" that could possibly be imposed upon a group like ours, all of us were knowledgeable observers who could probably figure out what we did not know for sure. There was also no question that we would be doing a lot of talking on TV in the weeks and months to come, which was why we had been invited. All the more reason, then, to avoid on-air speculation, especially if it involved obvious questions of operational security or troop safety. To illustrate, he talked about several things that were classified or sensitive and simply asked us to be careful. (At this, I shot a glance over at Dave Grange, but he can display an admirable poker face on such occasions.)

Rumsfeld and Myers had clearly taken a risk in telling us these things, but it had to be the safest bet in town. The nation's military had now been committed to battle, we were retired warriors whose sole relevance to that situation now consisted of explaining its highlights on TV, and the most senior members of our real profession had just asked us to be cautious; indeed, they had strongly suggested how important we were to their efforts. This was heady stuff at a moment when most of us would have reenlisted instantly just for the privilege of filling sandbags. The older and wiser among us kept such emotions under wraps and retained an objectivity that any professional journalist might have envied. Barry McCaffrey, who knew the terrain well from tank turret-top level, had particularly strong misgivings that the attacking force was too light, reservations that would soon put him at the center of controversy.

As if in warning, my thoughts kept returning to the writings of T. R. Fehrenbach, whose history of the Korean War contains an immortal line that Army officers are fond of quoting: "You may fly over a land forever; you may bomb it, atomize it, pulverize it and wipe it clean of life—but if you desire to defend it, protect it, and keep it for civilization, you must do this on the ground, the way the Roman legions did, by putting your young men into the mud."[18] A quarter-century's experience as a soldier and strategist had taught respect for those words, but there were also other voices, including some of Warden's disciples, arguing that it was "a moral imperative for an airman to avoid close combat." Fine, but the enemy always gets a vote too. So what happens when he copies the Vietcong tactic of grabbing you by the belt, so that your stand-off weapons become useless? In Iraq we were about to embark upon a trial by combat that, among other things, would demonstrate which school of thought was right.

[1] See the analysis by a future Secretary of Defense, William J. Perry, "Desert Storm and Deterrence," *Foreign Affairs* 70, no. 4, (1991): 66–82.

[2] John A. Warden III, *The Air Campaign* (Washington, DC: NDU Press, 1988), 39.

[3] The term is from Jeffrey T. Richelson, *The Wizards of Langley* (Boulder, CO: Westview Press, 2001).

[4] For a classic "systems analysis" view of these issues and terminology, see David S. Alberts et al., *Understanding Information Age Warfare* (Washington, DC: Department of Defense Command and Control Research Program, 2001). Available at http://www.dodccrp.org.

[5] Statement of Vice Adm. Arthur K. Cebrowski USN (ret.), Director, of Force Transformation, Office of the Secretary of Defense, before the Subcommittee of Defense, United States House of Representatives, Appropriations Committee, March 13, 2002.

[6] The integration of the Army's active and reserve forces into the so-called Total Force dated from the 1970s and the "Golden Handshake" agreement between Secretary of Defense James Schlesinger and legendary Army Chief of Staff Creighton Abrams. Of that agreement, borne out of bitter Vietnam experience, Abrams had said, "They're *never* going to take us to war again without calling up the reserves." Quote by James Kitfield, *Prodigal Soldiers* (Washington, DC: Brassey's, 1995), 149–51.

[7] Torie Clarke, *Lipstick on a Pig* (New York: Free Press, 2006), 58.

[8] In March 2006, General Trainor became even more widely known as the coauthor, with *New York Times* colleague Michael R. Gordon, of the best-selling book, *COBRA II: The Inside Story of the Invasion and Occupation of Iraq* (New York: Pantheon Books, 2006).

[9] Clarke, op.cit., 59.

[10] Eliot Cohen, *Supreme Command: Soldiers, Statesmen and Leadership in Wartime* (New York: Free Press, 2002), 209.

[11] Ibid., 213 (emphasis added).

[12] Shameless plug: Kenneth Allard, *Business as War* (New York: Wiley, 2004).

[13] To quote from the jacket copy of one of the more adulatory books of the genre. See Jeffrey Krames, *The Rumsfeld Way* (New York: McGraw-Hill, 2002).

[14] See, for example, Krames, 137–150 on "Acquiring and Using Intelligence," especially the "bad news" problem.

[15] John Arquilla and David Ronfeldt, *The Advent of Netwar* (Santa Monica, CA: RAND, 1996).

[16] Gordon and Trainor, op. cit., 95–96.

[17] Ibid., 99–100.

[18] T. R. Fehrenbach, *This Kind of War* (New York: Macmillan, 1963), 427.

CHAPTER SIX

Opening Night

· · · · ·

By March 2003, a recurring thought kept...well, recurring: that if military science had been a graduation requirement in any journalism school anywhere in the country, you might never have seen me on TV. Not only was the country engaged in the continuing war on terrorism, but the president looked more and more like a tongue-tied Texas Ranger every time the subject of Saddam Hussein came up in conversation. While the history of Desert Storm had not exactly repeated itself, a pretty good rerun was in progress. The volunteer army drawn from both active and reserve components had been assembled and ponderously transported to the Persian Gulf; it was now encamped close to the borders of Iraq, where its commitment to battle was expected any day. The military experts had been assembled as well, and at MSNBC headquarters just outside New York City, we were anxiously waiting for the countdown to end. We had worked with the production staff to help gather briefing books, equipment graphics, and maps. Based on what we knew from the Pentagon and our own sources, we had also told the staff as well as the top brass at MSNBC what we thought was the most likely plan of attack.

The lead expert in these latter briefings had naturally been Gen. Barry McCaffrey, who had commanded the 24th Mechanized Infantry Division in the first Gulf War. In those days he had been on the left side of the famous "Hail Mary" maneuver that Gen. Norman Schwarzkopf had used to deceive and then envelope the Iraqi forces occupying Kuwait. The division had driven straight north from Saudi Arabia to the Euphrates River valley, interdicting the Iraqi escape route back to Baghdad. That experience had left McCaffrey with an intimate knowledge of the very same terrain American forces would now have to cross to reach the Iraqi capital—a much greater distance than during Desert Storm. Although familiar with the new technologies and tactics that had steadily improved the American force ever since its lopsided victory more than a decade earlier, he also knew what might go wrong. In quiet but urgent tones, he now told the senior MSNBC staff what some of those things might be. Distance in the desert equaled a heavier demand on logistics of all kinds: the longer the journey the more food, water, ammunition, and fuel would be needed. Despite the high technologies involved in air support, weather was always an uncertainty.

But most of all he was concerned with what the Army calls the force-to-space ratio, meaning that there might not be enough combat power—troops, vehicles, firepower and momentum—to provide overwhelming force if the enemy chose to make a fight of it at any point along the route of attack. Had he been in charge, McCaffrey would have added at least one additional division to thicken the force. Equally important was an additional armored cavalry regiment of about five thousand soldiers and one hundred reconnaissance vehicles to provide security for the advance. Together with an additional military police brigade, the attackers would then have had ample forces to cover their advance all the way to Baghdad and secure the capital once it had fallen. A lifetime in combat had taught him not to underestimate the enemy, especially now that the Iraqis were fighting for the survival of the only nation many of them knew. There was dead silence in the room as Barry finished. Finally someone spoke up and said that most of them had always assumed the United States would win in a walk. We probably will, Barry responded, but you always have to be ready if the enemy proves tougher than you thought he might be.

Just over a month earlier, our counterparts—Gen. Wes Clark, Gen. Dave Grange, and Gen. Don Shepperd—had been called to CNN headquarters in Atlanta for a similar skull session. CNN, the granddaddy of the cable news networks, had risen to glory on the wings of the first Gulf War and was certainly not overawed by the careers of the distinguished gentlemen it had now contracted for informed commentary nor their seven collective stars. While always cordial, it was possible to detect an undercurrent of slight suspicion among the network stars who wondered if the analysts might be too pro-military for objective journalism. The anchors knew they needed help, but felt they had earned their spurs in the approved journalistic fashion and were after all *newspeople*. How very *unusual* to be asked to share the limelight with the unwashed, even high rankers, like these. Yet the anchors and the generals soon became a team because they needed one another as even the mighty CNN came to grips with the complexities of what promised to be a new kind of war. The working compromise seemed to be that the network wanted the generals to do well but that the anchors would remain the real stars, not the amiable new gentlemen who had merely worn stars on their shoulders.

Don Shepperd, who had piloted both commercial airliners and Air Force fighters, had served the network longest, gradually becoming accustomed to another CNN folkway: the somewhat disconcerting habit of the anchor taking an opposing view to anything said by the supposed experts. The Warheads were no exception to this contrarian tactic, which meant to highlight the truth on almost any issue. Still it took some getting used to when explaining that the sun rose in the east only to have the anchor furrow his brow and ask, "But, General, what do you say to those who argue that it all depends on one's perspective? And aren't you simply repeating again what Copernicus said so long ago?"

But on the eve of war, little one-upsmanship was visible in the meeting between the CNN Warheads and the network anchors, producers, and reporters. The generals explained how they expected the war to unfold and where the network's reporters might best station themselves in the conflict between good coverage and personal safety. Most important was what they should and should not say on the air. Broadcast live to both sides, CNN coverage was ubiquitous: live pictures of Iraqi scud missile strikes and American precision-guided-munition (PGM) attacks could quite conceivably be used to adjust this very long-range form of artillery fire. Thus it might be best to avoid saying things like, "Well, Miles, as you can see, that last Iraqi salvo didn't miss its target by very much. One minor adjustment to its range—probably even less than that in its deflection—and well, this entire oil terminal would now be ablaze. Back to you." Simple stuff, but exactly the kind of thing you have to drill into people constantly if they are to avoid making mistakes under the intense pressures of the media spotlight. And the cautions applied as much to the generals as the anchors.

Dave Grange went over the personal concerns he felt, based on what was known of the war plan. It was by now virtually certain that Turkey would not provide the landing, transit, and staging areas for the U.S. 4th Infantry Division, the strike force for the northern front of the Iraq invasion. Although other American units might provide diversions in the north, they would almost certainly be airborne or special forces, classic light infantry inserted directly by aircraft. While such tactics avoided the overland complication of offending Turkish sensitivities, there was no substitute for the armored and mechanized units of the 4th Infantry—one of the Army's best-equipped divisions—hammering down from the north while other Army and Marine Corps armored units provided an anvil by driving up from the south. Attacking from multiple directions was the way the Army liked doing things because it complicated the enemy's ability to concentrate his forces against any single axis of that attack.

Because that complication would now not exist, Dave was also worried about the "lightness" of the attacking force from the south, preferring that it be thickened with additional troops. However, like the northern front, this would not happen. Dave believed we would attack with what was there now, if only because the calendar and rising temperatures with the advent of summer spelled trouble for the American contingent. Now that they had been transported half a world away from their bases and logistical support, the choice was now to use them or to withdraw them. Saddam surely knew that too, and as the buildup reached a crescendo, the Americans sitting in their base camps on the Iraqi border would never present a better target for his missiles, artillery, or even suicide squads. With satellite reconnaissance an increasingly available commercial commodity—to say nothing of covert allies with their own capabilities—the only wonder was why Saddam had not yet attacked the Americans in their laagers. "It's called a spoiling attack and a competent enemy would do exactly that," Grange concluded. "Certainly the Russians, North Koreans, or even the Iranians would."

When Wes Clark stood to give his presentation, an understandable stir went through the audience. For months he had been taking positions that put him outside the prevailing consensus of military analysts. On the one hand, he disagreed with the doomsayers who predicted the Iraqis might make a stand in Baghdad recalling memories of Stalingrad—a nightmare scenario that some wags suggested meant only that the doomsayers knew little about either the Iraqis or Stalingrad. However, Wes had consistently maintained that war would be costly, was likely to disrupt the oil markets, and could commit the United States to billions in postwar reconstruction costs. He was also sharply critical of the Pentagon for attacking with a force less than half the size of what it should have been. Although the force in Kuwait supposedly numbered a quarter-million troops, 150,000 of them were navy, air force, and logistics personnel only indirectly involved in the ground campaign. Worse yet, the complications with Turkey had forced deployment adjustments that meant rerouting the 4th Infantry Division as well as other units through Kuwait; their equipment was either in transit, still being offloaded, or otherwise unavailable for immediate operations.

The only conceivable justification for these otherwise inexplicable glitches was that those advocating a "new kind of war" had carried the day over those old-school Army plodders who still believed in the "boots on the ground" theory of warfare. In a direct slap at Rumsfeld and the Transformation crowd, Wes suggested that he had heard these arguments before as NATO commander during the Kosovo campaign in 1999 when the airpower theorists endlessly argued that adding just five more targets to the air campaign would bring about decisive results. Similarly those same advocates were now hoping that Iraq would join Afghanistan on the "mission accomplished" roster and provide additional justification for shifting long-term resources away from the Army and toward the other services. But if the small margin for error proved too small or if a combination of weather and bad luck produced unforeseen complications, then heavy armored forces would be essential. In phrases he would soon repeat, not only on American television but also in European speeches and editorials:

> For when you are in battle, the neat logic of defense economics and the defense "professionals" is not much appreciated. You want everything you can get and you want it now—not a precisely calculated, new-kind-of, just-enough fight.[1]

I smiled after hearing those words, having known Wes for over twenty years and known about him for much longer. When he was commanding the Army's National Training center a decade earlier at Fort Irwin, California, I watched him outline our tactics in the offense for an audience of civilian academics—how we stressed the timed coordination of artillery, mortars, direct fire—even close air support. One of the academics raised her hand. "General, all that firepower. Somehow it really doesn't seem fair." "Ma'am," Wes had replied evenly, "we're the United States Army and we don't believe in giving the enemy the luxury of a fair fight." But now on the eve of the invasion it seemed as if we had spotted him a touchdown or two. Personally, I understood the reservations Wes had raised although there seemed little doubt about the outcome of the battle.

I thought our technology would give us an edge, but most of my confidence rested in the American soldiers comprising the attacking force. Together with their Marine, Air Force, and Navy partners, these troops had now benefited from a full generation of sustained professionalism, and it showed. The Iraqis might well make a stand somewhere on the way to Baghdad: but at least for the upcoming phase of this second war against Iraq, this was going to be Bambi versus Godzilla. After that it was anyone's guess. The Army chief of staff, Gen. Eric Shinseki, had only weeks before created a huge uproar when he told the Senate Armed Services Committee that "several hundred thousand" troops would be eventually needed to control postwar Iraq because of its size and history of ethnic tensions. Paul Wolfowitz, the deputy defense secretary, had disparaged Shinseki's estimate, calling it "wildly off the mark."[2] The truth was that no one really knew because the essence of warfare is uncertainty, or as my business audiences were regularly told, the enemy always gets a vote. That simple historical fact was why the Powell and Weinberger "doctrines" in force during most of the previous two decades had stressed the need to attack with more combat power than you thought might be needed but never anything less.

As I settled in for my shift at MSNBC one evening in late March 2003, the briefing books were updated, the maps posted, and everything seemingly in readiness.

With its own phalanx of reporters to draw from, the word around NBC News was that nothing was expected to happen for several more days. When it did, an aerial bombardment—"shock and awe"—would signal the start of the ground assault, much like the opening pistol shot of the Oklahoma Land Rush. There are two vital parts of the MSNBC complex. I had just left one: the MSNBC.COMmissary, famed for its culinary wizardry and one of the few places on the planet where chicken was served both as an entrée and as dessert. On the way back to my desk, I passed the second: the Network Operations Center, a glassed-in area with more than a hundred television monitors handling satellite "feeds" from all over the globe, like the electronics department at Wal-Mart but on steroids. The funny thing was, the news staff was now standing and pointing at the feeds from Baghdad, which were showing explosions interspersed with the wail of sirens and the staccato bap-bap-bap of anti-aircraft fire. As one explosion hit close to the camera, the picture momentarily dissolved into a white-yellow flash, prompting a chorus of "Whoas!" and "Oh, Baby!" So much for the conventional wisdom and any prospect of a quiet evening.

After six years with the network, including two wars and innumerable dustups, I knew my battle station when crises hit: I continued back to my studio desk, turned on the monitor, put my feet up, and tried to think carefully. That we were going to war was a simple fact that had been obvious for many months. Only weeks before, on the MSNBC simulcast of the *Imus in the Morning* radio show, I had argued that the pace of the American buildup suggested a race against time that could only be based on hard intelligence. Imus could be a tough interviewer, but the audience loved his tough, off-the-wall interrogations. But in any crisis I never faced either his questions or the MSNBC cameras without a strong sense that a lot of people were watching, including the real experts: Pentagon action officers, Department of Defense officials, and with the increasing reach of cable news, even warriors pretty close to the foxhole. After twenty-eight years in the profession of arms, these guys, rather than the news junkies, were my real reference group. They now knew the real story whereas I was just guessing, but it was important that those guesses reflect the soldier's expertise, judgment, and common sense.

The common sense thing was sometimes in especially short supply on cable TV. Steve the Producer now appeared over my shoulder with the first of the evening's many demands. "Well, is it 'shock and awe' yet, Colonel?" he asked insistently. "I mean, like, have you been following all these *huge* explosions that we're seeing now? Fox and CNN went live with it right away too. So is this the real deal or what? You've gotta tell us what's going on."

I turned away from the monitor and wondered again at the remarkable resistance that television producers displayed when confronted with any notion of subtlety. Instead their training, inclinations, and expertise simply favored transferring monkeys from their backs to yours as smoothly and quickly as possible. Monkey transference also occurred routinely in the intelligence officer's world, but there the weight of raw information might often tug you between two plausible and equally valid conclusions. In the world of cable news TV, the tension was often between "right," "right now," "right enough," and "what other networks are running this?" Such was apparently the case this evening, because between Steve and me, only one of us was concerned with some troubling ambiguities. The options were not promising, but sometimes you start with the simple things.

"OK, what time is it over there now?" I began.

"Ummm…about 5:30 AM?" he replied.

"So sun-up in Baghdad is less than an hour away," I said. "And that's when things get a little squirrelly for our team. We have the finest air force in the world, but they're like vampires: they mostly work at night because the Iraqis can't see us. And in the Iraqi air defense system, the worst thing you can do is asking anybody to turn on his radar set."

"But why is that?" he asked impatiently. "I thought the Air Force and the Iraqi gunners had been playing cat-and-mouse games for months over the no-fly zones."

"They have been," I replied. "But the game is over whenever the Iraqis try to illuminate one of our planes. 'Cause we have pilots who just *live* for the thrill of popping off an anti-radiation missile that rides the beam straight back where it came from. So unless our Iraqi air defender has a death wish, he leaves all that shiny new French electronic stuff in the OFF position."

"Well, how does all that change when the sun comes up?" he asked skeptically.

"For one thing, all our Stealth stuff is painted black," I explained. "Stands out against a cloud layer so the Iraqi gunners can see and track our guys optically: Stealth fighters, of course, but also B-2 bombers and anything else we have up there. The Iraqis may be low rent, but they have plenty of ammunition and it only takes one lucky silver bullet to bring down a very expensive aircraft. To say nothing of an even more expensive pilot."

True enough, but this was fast becoming a tutorial; much more of it and Steve's eyes would glaze over.

"So you don't think it's starting?" he asked anxiously.

"No," I concluded quickly. "It's a bit late in the evening for 'shock and awe' if it really is the kind of all-out bombing we expect. And we haven't heard anything about the ground assault either, so the timing seems out of whack there as well. Plus look at your monitor; you can still see buildings standing in Baghdad. It just doesn't add up right."

As if mocking my words, the monitor shook with the sight and sounds of another close-in explosion, punctuated by the frantic green blips of random Iraqi anti-aircraft fire. CNN and Fox News, as usual, were showing the same scenes we were. Two not very distinct eyebrows now resolved themselves into a single furrowed line as Steve the Producer pondered my words. This clearly was not what he had wanted to hear.

"Well, keep watching the network," he said. "And get ready. You're going to be in the chair with Lester Holt as soon as they come to us. And if we don't have a handle on what's going down over there, we're gonna look awfully stupid."

Although the producer's body language suggested departure, the ornery little bastard hadn't left yet. As with tiresome houseguests whose departures take forever, it was necessary to avoid the slightest movement that might have been misinterpreted as an invitation for more yadda-yadda. "Oh," he finally added as an afterthought, "one other thing. Whatever else happens, things are likely to start moving pretty fast. So if there are any questions you think we should be asking you, just jot them down and give them to one of the assistants. We'll either cue them up for Lester on the teleprompter or else just whisper them in his ear from the control room."

I nodded agreeably while suppressing the snorts of derision that would have sent the conversation into extra innings. Such overpreparation was simply unnecessary. Lester Holt is one of our savviest anchors and a military "brat" who always asks good questions. As the in-studio surrogate for the guy-on-the-couch at home, he was also a man with whom you could have a reasonable, relaxed, and intelligent conversation. But producers like Steve were always terrified that a hard-pressed anchor might have a momentary brain freeze that could turn into dead air, so they invariably tried to create "air blivets"—ten minutes of material crammed into a three-minute time slot. To help them, you worked with an assistant to figure out crisp questions that the anchor might reasonably ask, though they never, of course, wrote out your answers. You were simply expected to engineer one side of the conversation via teleprompter, deliver the other yourself off the top of your head, and do it all in those three minutes, kind of like expertise on a stick.

I still had my feet up on my desk in a back corner of the studio and purposely didn't move until after the producer had scurried off around the corner, because either in the military or on TV, you never let them see you sweat. Once he was safely gone, I savored the pleasure of his departure for only an instant before calling Jim Miklaszewski, NBC's ace Pentagon correspondent. I hated bothering him at such a moment, but nobody in Washington had better sources.

"Hey, Jim. It's Ken up at MS. Apologize for bothering you 'cause I know how busy you are right now, but can you give me a hint of what's going on out there tonight?"

"Plan's changed. Something's up. It's going down right now," Jim whispered hurriedly.

We didn't have time for a long conversation, so what "it" was still remained unclear. Later Jim told me that just after NBC Nightly News had aired that evening, he had called a White House source on an unrelated matter. In sonorous tones, the source then volunteered an unrelated fact of his own: "You know, of course, that the president will be addressing the nation this evening." Butter does not melt easily in the mouth of a Pentagon correspondent: "Oh, really," Jim replied smoothly, "and what's he going to be talking about?" From the sounds of the gunfire, it was pretty clear that the address would not include Social Security reform or the need to cut taxes.

But what we could see of the attack kept raising doubts in my mind, because it was a lot less than how "shock and awe" had been billed, even after you discounted the concept for the sophomoric nonsense that it was. Ceaselessly trumpeted over every media bullhorn, the overblown phrase had become firmly entrenched in the public's mind as the starting gun for the long-awaited American ground assault into the heart of Iraq. Massive air sorties were expected in this opening barrage: by some estimates, as many as three thousand GPS-guided JDAMs, cruise missiles, and laser-tracking smart bombs would rain down on "leadership targets" held dear by Saddam's regime. That wasn't happening here; so what was really going on?

We now saw President Bush on the monitors, his face drawn and tense, as he cryptically announced that "coalition forces" had begun striking "selected targets" and that the war had indeed begun. By then I was in the chair opposite Lester Holt, miked, wired, made up, and playing the role of "anchor buddy." Unlike the tightly scripted, three-minute hits of normal coverage, anchor buddy duties are what you mostly do during periods of breaking news. Depending on what's happening, you sit at the anchor desk or stand at the situation map until the producer and the stage manager collectively decide you're no longer needed. If that's twenty minutes or an hour or two, then that's what it is. (If you're at the map long enough and the coverage lingers, sometimes the stage manager may be kind enough to slide a bar stool over to you.)

But this kind of crisis coverage can actually be a lot of fun; because things are not so tightly packaged, there is more time to react in ways that can actually mimic a normal conversation between consenting adults. The reactions themselves are driven entirely by what is happening on the screen; because Bush would be ending his remarks any second, it was my last chance to give Lester a quick heads-up about what I had been able to find out.

"Be careful of the 'shock and awe' stuff: something's not quite right about it." I whispered, both our eyes watching the monitor to make sure that it was still the president's words that were going out over the air rather than our own.

"Hmph," sniffed Lester, his eyebrows rising. "What's wrong with it?"

"It's too light and too late to live up to the hype they've given it," I quickly replied.

"Think they've thrown in a little psychological ops or deception?" Lester asked.

"Maybe self-deception? Lot a that goin' around," I replied.

As Bush finished up with "and God *bless* America," Lester swung into his on-air routine just as smoothly as if we had all been there in the Oval Office.

There were no more opportunities to speculate about deception because we were now cast largely in the role of observers at a fireworks display, and with the show just about over. There were, of course, the endless replays of the earlier explosions; and with not much else to add, one had to resist inane comparisons: "Oooooooh, there goes a Roman candle and a starburst!" Being on camera means being on-stage. At such moments, you have neither comrades-in-arms, other video, the Internet, nor (unless the anchor chooses to read it to you on-camera as an improvisational gut check) the NBC News "hot file" with its most urgent bulletins. What you do have is all your military experience that has to be applied to incomplete, fragmentary, and possibly wrong information—another similarity to the life of an intelligence officer all over again. But rather than making careful judgments in closely caveated assessments and briefings prepared over many months, you are doing it on the fly, without a safety net and with millions of eyes watching to see if you succeed in making a fool of yourself.

The only way to survive is to concentrate, to focus your world down to that two-way conversation where you and the anchor are just two guys watching TV together.

Several times, Lester simply asked, "Colonel Allard, what are we seeing here and what do you think it might mean?" All you can do in that circumstance is to backpedal: describing for the audience what you think is occurring on-screen, putting it in some kind of sensible context, and resisting the urge to speculate much beyond that—what the military calls "staying in your lane." So I summarized:

> Lester, here is what we now know: the United States attacked Iraq tonight in what is certainly the opening act of a long-promised conflict. So we are at war. But what we don't know is whether the explosions and firing we have seen in Baghdad over the last several hours is the actual start of a campaign that some have called "shock and awe." Because what we're seeing, frankly, is a lot less than what some of those analysts have predicted.

Safe enough, but sometimes you just try and hit singles.

Things move pretty rapidly on TV, so there wasn't much time for reflection, but tonight's conversation with Lester came eerily close to Dick Cheney's description of what he had been doing the opening night of the first Persian Gulf War in 1991. The recollection was particularly memorable because it came during a speech at Washington's National War College, where I was serving as dean. Cheney, formerly the secretary of defense, was by this point just another rich-as-Croesus oil executive. He was candid, though, in admitting to the audience that what he had been doing that fateful night back in 1991 was just what most of the public was doing too: watching CNN. The difference, of course, was that he had the attack folder open in front of him and was checking off the televised explosions against the target lists. Same thing as with Lester and me the opening night of the second Gulf War: here is what should be happening if our guys are up there and doing it right.

But the more we watched, the more apparent it became that the fog of war was not lifting, despite everything that NBC News and the other networks could throw at the problem. Network feeds showed that the American ground contingent was stirring, but that the troops were still located pretty much where they had been before. It was becoming obvious that whatever "shock and awe" was, tonight was not going to be our night. Actually it was no longer night at all; by now our troops were probably applying their first layers of sunblock. What air attacks there were had now become sporadic and desultory. Off-screen, Steve the

Producer mouthed the words "shock and awe" and shrugged; I glared back. Lester was now wrapping things up for the audience at home, even as the in-studio stage crew visibly brightened as they sensed their long evening was about to end. Homes and hotel rooms beckoned because everyone from anchors to camera crew knew that the next day we would be hard at it again.

The real story began to emerge within hours: it turned out that the attacks of the previous evening had resulted from intelligence supposedly developed about another Saddam sighting, which the intelligence community seemed to develop with roughly the same frequency and reliability as Elvis sightings. While the intelligence turned out to be chimerical, the consequences were real enough. Two F-117 Stealth bombers had been diverted to attack this "target of opportunity" in the Dora Farms neighborhood in southern Baghdad with four 2,000-pound bombs. Although forty more Tomahawk cruise missiles had been added just for good measure, there was no sign that the attack had succeeded in decapitating the Iraqi leadership.[3] More strangely still, the air strikes had apparently come as a complete surprise to the Army, where the same televised images we had been watching were piped by public affairs officers into the tents of the waiting attack force. At the 101st Airborne Division, one officer later told embedded *Washington Post* reporter Rick Atkinson, "This is going to be a weird war. We're going to live it and watch it at the same time."[4]

The next night, Lester Holt and I were back again in our accustomed places, the fast-moving realities of televised combat momentarily overshadowing any reservations about doctrine or numbers. With the presidential announcement that hostilities had commenced, the ground attack had been moved up; there was early footage of combat engineers punching holes through the sand berms blocking the Iraqi border. An armored division on the move looks like your worst nightmare on the interstate, often stretching twenty miles or more from vanguard to rear elements. But nighttime in New York was dawn in Iraq, and the pictures of March 21–22 showed the forward elements of our ground forces moving to their attack positions. The video was transmitted to us live by our NBC "embeds"—network reporters attached at the hip to the combat units. The electronic immediacy of that arrangement was an unimaginable threat to operational security but further confirmation of the Pentagon's accurate assessment that good video equaled good politics.

It was surreal to be sitting next to Lester in our studio while we were talking back and forth via satellite video hookups to familiar correspondents like Kerry Sanders and Dr. Bob Arnot, their normally natty attire giving way to the "embed" combat gear of Kevlar helmets and flak vests. More familiar still was the figure of

David Bloom, a well-established NBC star with whom I had worked in both Washington and New York. Now riding through the Iraqi desert in his customized, all-terrain vehicle—the "Bloom-mobile"—David was providing our viewers with live, uncensored satellite video beamed directly from the fast-moving ground units. His pictures were stunning and gave our viewers a glimpse of something normally witnessed only by soldiers. Combat vehicles of every description—tanks, Bradley fighting vehicles, and Humvees—kicked up plumes of sand and dust as they roared north in combat array. The previous evening, there had been a lot of "Ken, what do you think we're seeing" kinds of questions as we watched the fireworks together. Not so now: here in broad daylight and in real time was the American armored juggernaut slashing toward the throat of its enemy.

When it was my turn to comment, there was a lot to say: "What we're seeing here now is nothing less than the ultimate commitment of American combat power. Not just an aircraft dropping bombs and flying away, but the American soldier with his rifle invading the territory of his enemy. Because when that soldier is committed, then the nation is too." God only knows, but in the heat of the moment, Fehrenbach may have slipped in there too.

"OK," Lester responded, "but when we make that commitment and a unit like the U.S. 3rd Infantry Division gets the order to march, what typically goes on? How do they carry out such a mission?"

"Lester, as stunning as these pictures are, they can only show our audience a piece of what that armored formation is actually doing. Cavalry and scout units are typically well in front of the column to smoke out enemy positions. On either side— and well out of camera range—we can expect flanking units to be deployed on both sides of the line of march. Artillery leapfrogs the formation as well, always keeping its guns within range just in case immediate 'fire missions' are called for."

Apache and scout helicopters now whizzed by, the noise of their rotors drowning out the voices of our correspondents. Lester chuckled, "More help from on high there, Colonel?"

"You bet," I replied. "That armored formation you're seeing is powerful, but the idea is to provide it with complete air cover. That means helicopters as well as jet fighters. As you know very well, between the Army and Air Force that means there are lots of ways for the enemy to experience 'death from above.'"

Some of that was pure BS, some of it sheer exhilaration that the waiting was over, and some of it simple relief that things for the moment seemed to be going well. The problem with being Lester's "anchor buddy" just now was that it was hard for any soldier to suppress his emotions or to even keep his voice normal. Because I had seen those armored formations on the move many times before, there was an overwhelming sense of what it had cost the nation to put those forces on the battlefield, not only the treasure expended but also the lives risked as our soldiers were committed to battle. But there is a visceral, even primeval, joy with which the warrior approaches combat: now watching "my guys" in the attack, a certain discipline was required just to avoid breaking into war cries.

But competing with those emotions was an even more pervasive sense of regret: that we had stopped short the first time and now had to go back; that competing theories of warfare would soon give way to the unpredictable effects of Murphy's Laws; that things would go inevitably and disastrously wrong, and when they did, soldiers would die. For good or ill, our young soldiers had now been put into the mud, or rather the same sands that had once seen Babylonian chariots, Greek hoplites, and Roman legionaries. Even a cursory look at military history suggested that our enemies, however befuddled for the moment by our Orgasmatrons of destruction, would recover and learn lessons. When they did, our press notices and PowerPoints would offer little protection against an opponent determined to take the fight to us and kill American soldiers in any way he could. It also took a concerted effort to explain to the TV audience that just the *environment* of the combat zone has inherent hazards that can snuff out a life as quickly and surely as a bullet.

At that moment—even in the heart of the media beast—you are supremely aware of what you don't know but strongly suspect. I looked up because now on the screen David Bloom was showing us a dirty, dusty, weary but still smiling American infantryman—probably carrying fifty pounds of gear in the desert heat. Although the face was unfamiliar, the grunt's uniform, weapons, and mission recalled a thousand memories of soldiers in arms; just for a second, I indulged those thoughts and emotions. It was the briefest of salutes, and after a few hard blinks I managed to return to the studio and the task at hand. Incredibly enough, now standing there just off-camera was Steve the Producer from the previous evening. I caught his eye, covered my mike, and as if aiming a pistol, pointed to the on-screen infantryman. "Hey, yo! You wanted to see shock and awe. Well, take a good look, because there he is."

From that moment until the fall of Baghdad was just over three weeks. By April 9, the Iraqi Republican Guard had been defeated, the regime had been toppled, and American units were effectively in control of the Iraqi capital.[5] In many ways, the pace of the campaign suggested Afghanistan, only now with much better video. Torie Clarke was primarily responsible, demonstrating the implications of her long-held belief that "the information age had changed military conflict forever." With seven hundred media "embeds" placed throughout the combat units, ostensibly in order to counteract the lies and propaganda of the Saddam regime, real-time combat footage flowed into American living rooms as never before. Everything had been tightly planned because "the world's understanding of the war would affect our ability to win it." Even individual targets were accompanied by a communications package prepared in advance to explain why it had been selected and collateral damage avoided. In a line that could have come out of the information warfare manuals I had worked on a decade earlier, the objective of this hyperactivity was described as *information dominance*: "The essence of the communication plan is to flood the zone with information."[6]

It worked. Just as Clarke and her colleagues had known all along, the videos showed to perfection the smart, often funny, occasionally profane, and superb young professionals of the armed forces. The openness and access helped even when things went wrong, as during the celebrated capture of Pvt. Jessica Lynch. The story did not play primarily as a screw-up caused when her unit got lost and ran into an Iraqi ambush. Instead it played to the pathos of an attractive female soldier subjected to the rigors of being a POW, punctuated by a dramatic rescue by special forces. The placing of the embeds had a further benefit because serving alongside the combat units inescapably created bonding, a tradition going back to great war reporters like Joe Galloway and Ernie Pyle. The reason is not difficult to understand: anyone placed in a position where his safety, sustenance, ability to perform his job, and such limited creature comforts as may be available depends on the good will of the combat soldier next to him usually develops a respect for that soldier bordering on reverence. And vice versa: witness the grief of their units when two of the most prominent media embeds—Michael Kelly of the *Washington Post* and David Bloom of NBC News—died in early April within a day of each other, accidental victims of that unforgiving combat environment.

Because of the media embeds, the spotlight inescapably shifted away from the Warheads throughout the rush to Baghdad. And for good reason because they were much closer to the scene than we were and had good video to boot. With all the video being generated, however, it seemed as if we had been recast as "color commentators" analyzing a football game and assessing how it might develop. In the rat-a-tat-tat of cable news format, MSNBC took to having the Warheads summarize battlefield events at least once every hour in "military minutes," which quickly came to resemble the Weather Channel more than a football game. We were often paired in swing shifts, and it became a kind of game to sort through the news wires to find something new to say, to master again the quirkiness of the screen-writer, to construct a coherently improvised narrative, and to wrap it all up in less than sixty seconds. (My personal best, with stage manager Tim Bender counting me down from off-camera, was fifty-eight and a tick, occasioning mutual high-fives and shouts of "You da man!" once we were clear.) One night, paired, with Col. John Warden, I pleaded with the producer for substance. "Why don't you give John and me three minutes to argue about airpower?" I asked, adding that Warden was one of its greatest modern advocates. Naturally she declined, but suggested we might try working some of those points into the confines of our regular one-minute segments. Far as I can recall, we never could.

The opportunities were sudden and fleeting, but covering the incoming combat footage provided some unforgettable moments. One of them came during the fight for Baghdad, when NBC cameraman Craig White filmed a medical unit accompanying 3rd Infantry Division soldiers sent to secure a strategic highway overpass. They were attacked by a Syrian unit fighting on the side of the Iraqis—and apparently determined to do so to the death. White's footage was dramatic—exploding vehicles, burning tanks, and all the detritus and carnage of close combat. But providing coherent commentary on a firefight is tough to do, especially when you're seeing it at precisely the same time as the anchor you're standing next to. Inevitably you focus on a few details, as when an Army private being treated for a leg wound rose up from his stretcher to squeeze off a burst from his M-16 at the attackers. This was no longer "shock and awe" but knee-in-the-gut, eye-gouging combat in a style the Romans would have instantly recognized.

White's footage was dramatic because you could actually see what was going on. Far more typical was the live video of a nighttime firefight one evening shortly after Americans took full control of Baghdad, though it was already tough to tell the difference between "die hards" and your Iraqi average looter.[7] We were preparing to wrap up an evening's coverage—all regular prime-time shows having been canceled for the duration—when firing broke out close to our Baghdad camera location. There was little that could be seen other than the odd muzzle flash or tracer round, yet we stood on the set opining endlessly about what "might" be happening on the ground eight thousand miles away, and for really only one reason: all our cable news counterparts were running precisely the same camera view as we were and with as little newsworthy information as we had. Eventually the producers tired of the game, our coverage ended, and we were sent back to our hotels. My buddy Lt. Col. Rick Francona had been on-camera with me and, as we pulled out our ear-pieces, he said, "Think CNN, Fox, and MSNBC could set up a hot line so we could negotiate a cease-fire on our coverage when it gets like this?"

The looting in Baghdad was an unsettling reminder that the debate on the number of American forces committed to the war had not permanently receded. In the first week of the campaign, there were numerous reports that overextended supply lines and Iraqi resistance had slowed the rate of advance—not surprising had you followed the prewar debate or even read any military history. Barry McCaffrey appeared on the *Today Show* to make the unexceptional point in public that he had already made in private during our Pentagon meetings: that the United States was relying on airpower to compensate for our deficiencies on the ground. However, both Rumsfeld and Joint Chiefs Chairman Gen. Richard Myers reacted immediately, strongly defending the war plan. Myers said, "It is not helpful to have these comments come out when we have troops in combat." Several weeks later, with U.S. troops now about to seize the Iraqi capital, Vice President Dick Cheney was speaking before a convention of the Veterans of Foreign Wars (VFW) to which he presumably had been invited as a guest, not ever having served in the military himself. Commenting on the success of the campaign, Cheney noted that "in the early days of the war, the plan was criticized by some retired military officers embedded in TV studios."[8]

He certainly meant McCaffrey and Wes Clark, but probably Jack Jacobs and me as well because all of us had voiced many of those same criticisms. I gave a characteristically starchy reply to the reporter who called that day for a comment: that Barry McCaffrey and Wes Clark had won many of the nation's highest awards for gallantry in combat compared to none at all for Dick Cheney or me. Therefore they had earned the right to comment as they chose and didn't have to go to the damned VFW convention on a guest pass either. But you cannot make critical comments on national television and be very surprised when the object of your criticism responds, plus the fact that all of the Warheads had made our living in a profession where the ass chewings were administered by experts who enjoyed their work. The controversy quickly faded from view except perhaps in the minds of those of us who had been involved.

So who was right? On the one hand, it is always difficult to argue with a win; but there will also be another day. On the other hand, the United States had triumphed over the Iraqis and had done so convincingly and after geopolitics had forced changes in its preferred campaign plan. The most worrisome concerns the Warheads had voiced were probably well founded but did not, in the end, come true. That was the good news: that we had successfully conquered Iraq, ended the regime of one of the most despotic dictators since Adolph Hitler, and given ordinary Iraqis the chance for a decent life. This was, of course, also the bad news, and for reasons that only Wes Clark had had the requisite vision, courage, and maybe just pure cussedness to articulate: several millennia of military experience suggest nothing so much as that war's outcomes are best written in pencil.

[1] Wesley K. Clark, "Battle Lines Drawn at Pentagon over New Kind of War," *The London Times*, March 20, 2003.

[2] See Associated Press, "Army Chief: Occupying Force Could Number Hundreds of Thousands," February 25, 2005; and Eric Schmitt, "Pentagon Contradicts General on Iraq Occupation Force's Size," *New York Times*, February 28, 2003.

[3] The complete story of the attack on Dora Farms is told by Gordon and Trainor, op. cit., 164–81.

[4] Quoted by Rick Atkinson, *In the Company of Soldiers* (New York: Henry Holt, 2004), 103–4.

[5] For three compelling in-depth accounts of the campaign to capture Baghdad, see Atkinson, op. cit; David Zucchino, *Thunder Run* (New York: Grove Press, 2004); and Evan Wright, *Generation Kill* (New York: Penguin, 2004). The most comprehensive history of that campaign yet to emerge is by Michael Gordon and Bernard Trainor, *COBRA II* op. cit.

[6] Torie Clarke, *Lipstick on a Pig* (New York: Free Press, 2006), 54–55.

[7] Craig White's account of that firefight is in *Operation Iraqi Freedom*, published by NBC News (Kansas City: McMeel, 2003), 169–74.

[8] The "war of words" controversy and the referenced quotations are in NBC News, op. cit., 77–80.

CHAPTER SEVEN

2004: The Media and the Election That Decided Nothing

• • • • •

The American presidential election of 2004 may be remembered for many things by future historians, but for the Warheads it would become a byword for what was not discussed. Like the dog that did not bark, this first presidential election since the country was plunged into war after 9-11 was chiefly remarkable for how little serious discussion took place about how to win that war, what strategy would be pursued to achieve that end, and even more critically, what resources the nation might expect to commit in achieving these aims. Instead of debating issues like military manpower, the demands of counterinsurgency strategy, and how those demands might be supported and shared more equitably by the American people, the Warheads found themselves involved habitually in less strategic but far more "newsworthy" ponderings; worse yet, they were sometimes drawn into insane discussions about the service records of the candidates from thirty years earlier. Far from being a referendum on Iraq and the global war on terror, the election of 2004 sometimes descended into a needless opening of Vietnam-era scar tissue and the airing of issues long since buried if not entirely resolved.

Yet new and more troubling issues persisted. At his confirmation as the incoming head of the U.S. Central Command (CENTCOM) the previous year, Gen. John Abizaid had the temerity to suggest that the ongoing resistance in Iraq was the work of insurgents rather than "dead-enders" or "die hards," prompting a rash of shushing not heard in Washington since Monica Lewinsky said she had it in mind to tell the truth. Donald Rumsfeld let it be known that he was none too pleased with Abizaid's characterization and did not use that term himself until almost a year later. Late in 2003, the capture of Saddam Hussein was triumphantly announced—"We got him!"—by the head of the "Coalition Provisional Authority," U.S. Ambassador Paul Bremer. Surely, it was thought, this must finally be a sign of progress.

In a fit of excitement, MSNBC recalled the analysts, and we had to slog through an early Washington snowstorm to entrain for Secaucus. The problem was that the capture was at best a twenty-four-hour story. Once the details of the apprehension had been covered repeatedly and a few analytical guesses hazarded about the implications of the Great Event, well, there was very little to do. Coverage lagged until the NBC News Prop Department hit on the brilliant idea of replicating the "spider hole" that had served as Saddam's hiding place. After its obligatory first-run appearance on NBC, the replica was trucked over to New Jersey and with great fanfare reassembled on our sound stage. The prop was little more than interlocking boxes made from heavy-gauge plywood, but it provided a reasonable backdrop for several discussions between me and our afternoon anchor, Contessa Brewer. The fun soon ended and, in the usual fashion, so did our temporary stint in Secaucus. A week or so later, I took a phone call from my daughter who was attending her first year of college at the time. "Hey, I saw you on TV," she began. "Real TV too, not just MSNBC. The Comedy Channel." It turned out that Jon Stewart had chosen Contessa and me as the objects for his nightly fun, taking special delight in skewering my use of the term "hidey-hole" and wondering how much they paid us. Not enough, obviously.

Laughter was a commodity that would be in increasingly short supply as the capture of Saddam failed to end the insurgency. Instead new names like Abu Musab al-Zarqawi came to be learned and feared, the chieftain for the Al Qaida network in Iraq becoming second only to Bin Laden as the world's "most wanted" terrorist. Although 2004 had begun with new excesses in Superbowl frippery, the war would become the essential backdrop to nearly every other story, the elephant at the garden party that could never be entirely ignored. In its "State of the News Media" report for 2004, Journalism.org found that there was more coverage in a typical sixteen-hour cable news day devoted to reporting of the war in Iraq war (2 hours, 17 minutes) than for politics in the presidential election year (1 hour, 35 minutes).[1] So with all this coverage, how can it be argued that the most critical issues of the war had little or no impact on the electoral campaign of 2004? The explanation is simple: each of the three institutions most concerned—the media, the military, and the government—was absorbed either in coping or simply in promoting internal agendas, running full tilt on tracks that only sometimes intersected.

Of the three, government was the institution with the clearest sense of mission: elect a president in the 2004 edition of our quadrennial sweepstakes. For the Republicans, the stakes were clearer yet: four more years for George W. Bush. Winning became identical with defending the president's record on Iraq and the war on terror against all comers. For the Democrats, things were characteristically ambiguous. A deep-seated distrust and an instinctive distaste for all things military had been imprinted in the Democratic DNA ever since the Vietnam War. When the Democrats gathered in Boston for their convention in late July, the *New York Times* would report that nine of every ten delegates opposed the war and thought any gains were not worth the price in American lives.[2] The riddle they were stuck with—and never really solved—was how to criticize the war without criticizing the troops. No such careful distinctions had applied during Vietnam, but now the rapidly aging lefties seemed trapped in their own time warp.

To them Wes Clark initially seemed like a godsend. He had formally entered the presidential race the previous September, the *New Yorker* declaring that "he was the anointed choice of many in the Clinton wing of the Party, the stop-Dean candidate charged with keeping Democrats tethered to the center." And for many other Democrats, a kind of uniformed talisman, "a tool for neutralizing George Bush's perceived strength on national defense." But the fulsome praise of that article had also carried the critical comments of two other retired generals, including Gen. Hugh Shelton, the former Chairman of the Joint Chiefs. Shelton, in particular, had weighed in with some especially tough judgments about why Clark had been retired early from his position as supreme NATO commander: "I will tell you the reason he came out of Europe early had to do with integrity and character issues, things that are very near and dear to my heart....Wes won't get my vote."[3]

It was an "I told you so" kind of moment, although this was something you would never say to a friend. Before he entered the ring, I had simply reminded Wes of something that had occurred back in the mid-'90s when there was a boomlet of support for a Colin Powell presidential candidacy. I had attended a typically Washington-style symposium where policy wonks and practitioners noodle endlessly over those "if-ya, could-ya, would-ya" kinds of questions, this time speculating on the implications if Powell ran for president. That night, famed *Washington Post* writer Bob Woodward had been one of those practitioners and his words were chilling: if Powell actually ran, then he would come under the kind of scrutiny from which he had thus far been exempt. In particular, his Vietnam service record "would become Powell's Arkansas"—this a reference to the Whitewater investigations that had bedeviled Bill Clinton. For his own reasons, Powell had later decided not to run—a move that many of us fully understood. "Wes, we both know General Powell and respect him," I said. "He was also the first black officer to become chairman of the Joint Chiefs of Staff, the man credited with winning Desert Storm. And they were going to put him under a microscope. Do you have any idea what they will do to you?"

Wes listened politely, thanked me, and then, of course, entered the campaign knowing full well what he would face and from far more knowledgeable advisers than me. The standard rap on him was that he was tightly wound, an ambitious, highly politicized general who could sometimes be tough for superiors and subordinates to deal with. After his candidacy had been announced, one of the first calls I fielded was from Jonathan Alter of *Newsweek*, who asked, "Is it really true that General Clark is considered the Eddie Haskell of the officer corps?" I laughed, of course, because you could probably make that argument or, if you wanted to, ruminate on his flaws. But you could not argue with his extraordinary talents nor fault the man's courage; and even if you disagreed with what he said, you had to admire the force and cogency of his views. He had by now published another book, *Winning Modern War*, and its message was clearly meant to resonate in 2004:

> In fact, the Bush administration's focus on Iraq [has] weakened our counterterrorist efforts, diverting attention, resources, and leadership, alienating allied supporters, and serving as a rallying point for anyone wishing harm to the United States and Americans....Osama bin Laden and his followers could have hoped for nothing more than another U.S. attack on an Islamic state to rouse popular enthusiasm and recruit the next wave of terrorists. By mid-August 2003 the Saudi government reported that 3,000 of its citizens had "disappeared," apparently over the border to Iraq, drawn to the opportunity to engage the Americans at close range on their own ground.[4]

But by late spring, it had become apparent that the nomination would go to John Kerry, one of the few Democratic leaders other than Wes to have a distinguished war record, although even that rapidly came under fire as the campaign wore on. Another CNN colleague, Ret. Lt. Gen. Dan Christman, then joined Wes as an adviser to the Kerry campaign. A former West Point superintendent, Dan was thereafter accosted by classmates when he attended his own Academy reunion. "How could you possibly be supporting Kerry?" they demanded. Here we were at war and whatever could Dan mean by suggesting that it might be acceptable for military officers to vote for...those people? "Do you have any idea what is happening to this Army we love?" Dan replied. He added that the manpower controversy in Iraq was only one symptom of its problems; officer attrition and recruiting shortfalls were others. Added together the conclusion was unmistakable: unless policies were changed, the force was rapidly headed back to the bad old "hollow Army" days that had afflicted the service after Vietnam.

Larger numbers of the Army alumni than one might have expected understood instinctively that something was wrong, but things had not yet progressed to the point that they were ready to jump the good ship George W. They, indeed, remembered the days of the hollow Army under Jimmy Carter, and remembered as well that the Army had not completely recovered until after Ronald Reagan had finally upped its pay scales: thereafter the volunteer force had rapidly transitioned into the professional force that had triumphed in Desert Storm. Somewhere in that transition, the strongly pro-defense "Scoop Jackson" wing of the Democratic Party had largely vanished. Retirement or mortality had removed its few remaining stalwarts like Sam Nunn in the Senate and Bill Nichols in the House from the congressional ranks. With no obvious replacements stepping forward to fill their shoes, there was a resulting leadership vacuum that left Democrats utterly disconnected from the national security consensus that had become an instinctive part of American life after 9-11. Yet most Democrats appeared utterly indifferent to the gap; on the eve of the election, party stalwarts in one New York suburb wondered what had become of the traditional presidential campaign and its focus on jobs, health care, poverty, and prescription drug prices.[5]

As with almost every political or economic issue, everything affects everything else. In 2004, this roadblock powerfully affected the second major American institution—the media—and restricted its ability to uncover and report on the war's most important realities. Without powerful congressional leaders to stir things up, schedule hearings, write op-eds, and accept bookings on Chris Matthews to get in a few on-air harrumphs, reporters had little reason to become more involved in the minutia of issues they perceived only dimly as generalists. This was especially true with the hard-core issues that in 2004 were affecting the forces in Iraq; manpower, resources, and the slow adaptation to what was becoming full-blown insurgency warfare. And yet there was little obvious demand from Congress or the public to delve more deeply into these issues so that reporters had few footholds from which to begin. Because popularity equals dollars, and because reporters are members of profit-making organizations with ever-keener eyes on the bottom line, it was not surprising that news organizations similarly tended to shift their attention elsewhere. Reason also to appreciate two closely related facts of the information age: that the media does not so much lead public opinion as follow it; and that the explosive growth in the means to distribute information even makes the term "media" highly suspect.

Whatever it meant to be members of the "media," only a fraction of the original seven hundred "embeds" were still working as reporters in Iraq. They occasionally joined the combat units for brief tours but mostly did "stand-ups"—providing live feeds back to the network to give a brief perspective on breaking news—but clearly the era of good feeling was over. Partly to blame were the very real threats to personal safety posed by the insurgency as well as by the ever-more-lethal environment. Even though it was in Baghdad's supposedly secure "Green Zone," NBC Pentagon correspondent Jim Miklaszewski had accompanied Deputy

Defense Secretary Paul Wolfowitz during an October 2003 visit to Baghdad when insurgents got close to the hotel housing the VIPs and fired rockets. The barrage barely missed Jim, who nevertheless retained his sense of humor, vowing he would never again stay at the Maison Wolfowitz, where the management tolerated such lax security and the wine list was so ordinary.

Back at MSNBC, there were subtle signs that interests had shifted. For one thing, our photo montage of American heroes had been shifted to a less conspicuous wall in the studio where it was now well out of camera range. During the long buildup to Iraq, MSNBC viewers had been invited to send in letters and photographs of sons, daughters, husbands, wives, and miscellaneous sweethearts gone off to war. Eventually the correspondence reached over a thousand, took up three walls, and was offset by a brace of teddy bears clad in battle dress uniforms (BDUs) and sporting yellow ribbons. Some were funny, many were touching, but all represented an absent loved one, usually profiled on the air in regular segments by anchors like Natalie Morales. The segments were shamelessly sentimental, but they were a nice tie-in to what the home audiences were feeling. But now the wall of heroes, the war room, and even our topographic map had all been shifted to make way for coverage of the many stories arising from the trials and travails of Michael Jackson and Kobe Bryant. Other grotesqueries beckoned as well, such as the gruesome and bizarre murder investigation of Laci Peterson. In an excess of loyalty over common sense, one staffer told me, "I feel sorry for the people involved, of course, but this case came at just the right time for the network. We needed another issue besides the war."

Human interest always sells, but cable TV's coverage of celebrity justice and murder investigations hardly meant that ordinary Americans were thus deprived of in-depth coverage concerning the key issues in Iraq. Far from it, given the barrage of other electronic media including broadcast news as well as those utterly obsolete technological throwbacks such as books, journals, magazines, and newspapers. Instead, the Warhead experience may be significant for what it says about how Americans are absorbing information about the war their nation is currently prosecuting, especially because so few of our fellow citizens had any personal understanding of what war is really all about. Yet in 2004, cable TV brought to the average viewer in an average day over two hours of programming on the Iraq war. So where did it go? In its back-to-back surveys for 2004–5, the respected Journalism.org, a branch of the Pew Research Center for the People and the Press, reached the following conclusions:

- That while cable TV "has now reached adulthood," because of its convenience, it is immediate, overwhelmingly repetitive, and dominated by live, stand-up interviews.

- That while cable TV is increasingly trusted as a medium available from personal digital assistants (PDAs) to airport waiting rooms, "the content of cable news is measurably thinner, more opinionated, and less densely sourced than other forms of national news."

- That while there are some differences among the three major cable news networks, it is the similarities that stand out, not only in what they choose to cover but also in how they do it.

- Finally, in what must be a Comedy Channel-class understatement, "The menu of topics that get substantive coverage on cable [TV] is fairly narrow."[6]

In 2004, there were three continuing stories being regularly visited and revisited on the Jumbotrons of the Electronic Coliseum:

1. *American casualties:* Surpassing the first thousand in 2004, this story was constantly rehearsed not only with the daily casualty count but every time a helicopter crash or a devastating explosion caused a particularly bad jump in the American death toll.

2. *The prisoner maltreatment scandal at Abu Ghraib:* Pandering to the worst impulses in journalism and profoundly shocking a large international audience, Abu Ghraib was undeniably sensational and the most severe blow to American military leadership since 9-11. Because many of the guards were reservists, it may have ultimately said more about U.S. prisons than the U.S. Army.

3. *The growth of the insurgency:* Although the two battles for Fallujah became the year's bookend events, it was difficult to relate individual engagements to the larger picture of how well the American forces were adapting to what was by now a full-blown insurgency. Similarly problematic was tying those events into the larger issue of the American will to win.

If there is a single complaint universally voiced by every Warhead across all three networks, it is the lack of airtime devoted to what all of us believe are some fundamentally important issues. This is, of course, just another way of asking: Why aren't we on more? The answer is that, every time we are, a compromise has been struck by our networks between the various costs of an appearance and the need to cover airtime. The expenses are not cheap and can include booking, two-way transportation, makeup, studio overhead, satellite time, even lodging and meals if multiple hits are planned across several days. While the most economical solution is to use taped replays of these hits several times in the course of a day, they usually have a much shorter shelf life due to breaking news, but even more to the need to keep the audience interested. Maintaining audience interest is the rule governing almost everything else in cable news because no producer ever forgets that the audience is armed with remote controls. For that reason, the received wisdom is that audience attention span is best measured in three-minute increments: in effect, a nation of soft-boiled eggs.

While some segments can run longer, it is simply assumed that keeping things moving quickly is the only way to ensure that the audience does not lose interest. If it does, the network ultimately suffers a loss in ratings and profits. No wonder then that the Warheads are nothing if not succinct because it simply goes with the territory. With the insurgency, however, Rick Francona started noticing several worrisome patterns. For one thing, the United States seemed to be telegraphing its moves every time a major insurgent stronghold appeared to be developing. When those attacks finally took place, the American forces would sally forth from their base camps, engage the enemy, secure the area, and then return to their base camps. This had been a classic mistake of the Vietnam War: all of us trained in counterinsurgency recognized it and understood that here was yet another manifestation of the chronic shortage of American soldier power. But in three minutes or less there was almost no way to connect all those dots. Often one of us would try and "sell" a producer on a story, especially if there was good video to go along with it. But decisions often turned on the judgment of whether the anchor and the Warhead could sensibly lay out the issue, coming to a reasonable conclusion in three minutes and, as a producer airily put it on one occasion, without sounding like you're both out of breath.

Tall order and another reason why little in-depth coverage was routinely attempted on cable TV, a point also made by the Pew Center survey which noted the scant coverage of any story not surfaced by headline coverage.[7] Dave Grange almost resigned his position with CNN out of sheer frustration with the way the network covered every other aspect of a story—and in fact repeated it over and over again—but frequently ignored the why and the how. Format and time restrictions were usually cited as reasons a story was turned down, but Dave would still try to seed the right questions when calling to suggest an angle. If he was successful in generating some interest, a booker would usually call back first and the outline of a story would be fitted into a time slot. Next, an assistant producer would call back for "pre-tape interview," and Dave would shape a general story line into the specific questions that would guide the interview. Shortly before airtime, it was not uncommon for the senior producer, who worked directly for the anchor, to call as well, often beginning with the words, "We just heard...." Sometimes it was possible to keep the story on point and sometimes not, but when you got on-air with the anchor, all bets were off. Then it was a matter of personal chemistry, the bond that had been established between anchor and analyst, and wherever the anchor felt like taking the story. When Aaron Brown asked three variations of a question Grange felt violated the operational security of U.S. special forces, he got three consecutive nonresponses and never invited the general to return. No problem because other anchors soon took up the slack.

Most of us on the other networks assumed that Fox gave its military analysts considerably more latitude. As the Pew Research Center noted in 2004, while the audiences for other cable networks had been flat, the Fox audience share had grown by half, outstripping CNN. Most of that gain had come from political conservatives and Republicans, who now had made Fox their network of choice; much of that loyalty presumably stemmed from the work of the Fox military analysts.[8] In early 2004, Paul Vallely and Tom McInerny wrote a book, *Endgame*, that was almost an exact counterpoint to the one authored by Wes Clark:

> Despite the best wishes of some, the Web of Terror cannot be talked to death, no "peace process" will work, no foreign aid will suffice unless the countries involved make a commitment...to forgo jihad, forgo terrorism, forgo weapons of mass destruction. Countries that will not do this willingly must be compelled to do it. Terrorism and the proliferation of weapons of mass destruction are not something we have to live with; they are something that the rogue states of the Web of Terror have to live without.[9]

However, ideology made very little difference as these generals were no more successful with Fox than Clark had been with the Democrats because complex questions of strategy were no easier to discuss in a three-minute Fox segment than in a three-minute hit on CNN or MSNBC. All of us were being aced out by the quick hit, the lurid story (hopefully with video), or the one where all the dots were neatly lined up; anything else was usually a very tough sell.

Who was making these decisions? The 2004 media survey had some thoughts on that as well:

> The dominant impression is that managers in the control room rather than on-air talent, function as the real agents of influence in cable. They decide what pictures to air, what stories to cover, where to go next, who gets to express expert knowledge and analysis. They define the personality of the product....On cable, whoever runs the

control room is the star, more than the anchor [and] certainly more
than the correspondent-producer team gathering news in the field.[10]

The Warheads knew exactly who these people were because all of us had seen
them in one incarnation or other. They were the battalion commanders of cable
news, the adult supervision held responsible for whole time blocks ("I've got the
2 to 4 today") during the day or primetime shows in the evening. They were the
thirty-somethings, smarter than the average bear, perpetually in the middle of a
gaggle of more junior staffers, sometimes huddling with the anchor, and now
mysteriously vanishing into the Twilight Zone of the Control Room, where they
were indeed in godlike control of who said what, where, and for how long. And
when Dave Grange, Tom McInerny, Rick Francona, or any of the rest of us were
trying to sell a story to the network, these were the people to whom we went
cap in hand.

These folks had one other thing in common—a complete absence of any personal
military service—although it would have been churlish as well as stupid to have
alluded to that fact when you were in the middle of telling them you were working a story that would fit perfectly into the next hour's "A block." Their lack of
military experience did not, of course, make them bad people; for reasons
explored earlier in this book, they were simply the latest products of a generation
in which the whole notion of military service had been systematically bred out
like some unwanted genetic trait. But ignorance has its own failure chain: these
people were now controlling what got on the air and their programmed inexpe-
rience made it that much more difficult for us to connect the dots for them. This
was true whenever Wayne Downing or Rick Francona were trying to give them a
one-minute crash course in counterinsurgency, what the United States appeared
to be doing wrong at Fallujah, and how we might combine those insights with
that newly arrived video of the latest explosions. Depending on how well their
considerable sales skills were working that morning—or simply if there was an
unanticipated hole in the programming—"the senior" might buy off on the segment concept and the hit would air.

When faced with a decision on coverage of a story, however, the senior producers often turned to journalists like themselves—or like the journalists they
secretly aspired to become. More than once, I was thrown in front of the cameras
when news suddenly broke on an issue that was well within my range either as
a soldier, an author, or simply as an analyst who had been around the network
for a few years. In November 2005, for example, one of the three hotels bombed
by Al Qaida in Amman, Jordan, just happened to be one where I had stayed on
an official visit ten years before. Not much to go on, of course, but a reasonable

starting point—particularly if one had worked terrorist bombings, first as a badge-carrying investigator and then as a TV analyst.

The drill for the analysts was almost invariable: react to the event, put it in a reasonable context for the audience, and pass hastily written notes or any other timely cues to whatever anchor happened to be on at the moment. It was actually exhilarating while it lasted; but usually the Warheads would be preempted within minutes, their expertise suddenly dispensed with. By then the bookers would have done their work and marshaled a suitable assemblage of reporters to offer their thoughts—profound and otherwise—to the TV audience. Reporters from the *Times*, the *Monitor*, the *Post*, the *Journal*, *Roll Call*, *Time*, and *Newsweek*—all were interchangeable—and all contributed regularly to "the media interviewing media" phenomenon.

Talented and able people, of course, but you could see why Dave Grange had become so pissed off over at CNN because those same shortcomings bedeviled the rest of us too. The reporters' emphasis was always on the who, the what, the where, and the when—but seldom on the all-important issues of *why and how*. The latter were those connect-the-dots questions, which could rarely be compressed into the three-minute, attention-grabbing format of cable news. Much the same thing was unfortunately true when it involved our reporters on the scene in Baghdad, where NBC correspondents like Ned Colt and Jim Maceda showed impressive courage and dedication on assignments putting them in harm's way.

The losses of David Bloom and Michael Kelly during the invasion had been ominous portents as the risk for reporters continued apace with the fast-growing insurgency. By 2006, network stars like Bob Woodruff of ABC and Kimberly Dozier of CBS would be severely wounded in IED attacks, surviving, in part, because of the state-of-the-art combat medical care by the Army's "Baghdad ER." Even so, they were the lucky ones: just after Dozier was wounded, the Committee for the Protection of Journalists reported that seventy-one journalists had been killed since March 2003—more than either Vietnam or World War II.[11]

It was that kind of war, of course, with no frontlines or neat, linear boundaries behind which a reporter might reasonably seek a degree of protection while trying to cover an inherently dangerous story. While there simply was no way to cover the Iraq story safely, or even to leave the fortified news compounds in Baghdad without private security convoys, the correspondents often seemed to be putting themselves at risk for paltry results. Their "hits" were governed by the same three-minute limitations as almost everything else on cable news and usually incorporated the standard guidance of local news outlets that "if it bleeds, it leads." Not surprisingly, explosions, death, and mayhem dominated most coverage. While Rumsfeld and the entire panoply of conservative talk radio habitually complained that "the media" was concentrating exclusively on the bad news, the reality was that the bad news was usually accompanied by better video—so that's what got on TV. But for no more than three minutes at a time, lest the audience of military illiterates at home in the Electronic Coliseum become bored and change the channel.

Their lack of understanding translated to a lack of demand for connect-the-dots kinds of stories; in turn, such profound audience disinterest shaped everyday programming choices made by the senior producers at every network. At least until a story like Abu Ghraib came along and removed all ambiguity. Then the challenge was not getting on-air because the story had seemingly been created to ensure the continued full employment of the Warheads. Instead the task was to get beyond the obvious sensationalism of those gag-making digital photographs, to get the producers and anchors to pose questions beyond the usual inane barrage. One of the first questions I was able to insert into an interview was why, with a Pentagon so hopped up on using information operations with every story, had none of the senior Pentagon officials anticipated something so ordinary as troops with digital cameras? Far from being shocked, why did they not anticipate the likelihood of such a thing happening? If you write such questions to be used on TV, then you had best have a ready answer. Mine was that the Internet and digital imagery had merely provided new means for the troops to do what they had always done—tell mom, dad, the newspaper, and the local member of Congress what they had been up to lately. Information operations did not take place on a one-way thoroughfare and what was happening here to those Pentagon officials was covered by a brand-new twenty-first-century term: blowback.

There were other issues connected with Abu Ghraib as well. But the one that mattered most to me was what the incident said about the adequacy of the training of reserves prior to their deployment—yet another aspect of the manpower story. I knew about training interrogators, having both commanded them and supervised their training at the Army Intelligence Center in Arizona decades before. What had happened at Abu Ghraib was the antithesis of everything we had taught our trainees, instruction that routinely emphasized the need to "get inside the opponent's head," as distinct from simply whipping his ass, which is pretty much what had happened over there. The sexual shenanigans had been even more out of control, the kind of thing for which we routinely put soldiers in front of a court-martial. What had happened here? Much of the Army's rebuilding and rebirth after Vietnam resulted from a revolution in our training, particularly its systematic integration into the tasks expected in combat. Was the manpower crunch now starting to erode what had been so carefully constructed over three decades?

The Warheads were regularly given opportunities to interview "senior defense officials" via long-distance conference calls that operated under the same not-for-attribution ground rules as our Pentagon meetings. Not long after the scandal had broken, a call was arranged with a senior intelligence officer who had been one of my War College students. He was a genuinely nice guy and a highly capable young officer, and it was obvious even back then he was headed for the stars; now he wore two of them. "General, good to be with you, even by phone. Congratulations on the star. Now what in the world were your people doing over there? Didn't they remember *anything* we taught them?" Naturally there weren't any good answers, and even if there had been it was not clear how we could get any of that stuff on the air. I could just imagine the video they would probably use too—the grainy photo of that idiot Spec. Four with the Alfred E. Newman grin and her foot on a miserable Iraqi POW. I sighed and the conference call soon ended.

It was no use. The Defense Department and the Army had immediately started empanelling various boards of investigation—nine separate ones by some estimates—in the same way that an octopus squirts out ink when it feels threatened. The funny thing was that those boards never seemed to recommend charges against the higher levels of the chain of command responsible for the working conditions under which Abu Ghraib operated, just the junior enlisted people. Rumsfeld had submitted his resignation twice, only to have it rejected both times by President Bush, who then "admonished" the defense secretary.[12] Thereafter, Rumsfeld took to minimizing the incident as the work of a few members of a single swing shift of prison guards. Well, maybe so, but that single shift had gone farther than any Al Qaida hit squad ever invented to undermine the legitimacy of the American war effort—in Iraq and elsewhere in the Middle East.

There was also a certain irony because at the time I was reading the *Flyboys*, James Brady's gripping account of World War II naval aviators, including the elder George Bush who had been shot down on a bombing mission over the Japanese-held island of Chichi Jima. He was fortunate to have escaped capture because, as Brady's book shows all too clearly, Japanese soldiers were not only killing American prisoners but subjecting their bodies to ritualized cannibalism.[13] It might have been an aberration by a single swing shift, but that did not stop the United States from tracing the responsibility for those incidents all the way up the chain of command—not just down. And properly so, because there is a lot of military history underlining the need to recognize what can happen when good soldiers are tired, scared, bored, frustrated, and uncomfortable, and guarding prisoners who are even worse off than they are.

The real significance of Abu Ghraib for me was that it provided the first unmistakable indicator that the United States might be in more trouble in Iraq than anyone yet knew. The scandal broke in March: in September, just before the U.S. presidential election, an article appeared in the prestigious journal *Foreign Affairs*, which went a long way to summarize where things really failed. Its author, Larry Diamond, a Hoover Institution scholar and a former adviser to Ambassador Bremer, argued that "hubris and ideology" had led the administration to reject military advice and occupy Iraq with a force far too light for its task—only a fraction of the 300,000 that might have been adequate. The failure could even be traced back to the invasion when the attackers had been strong enough to seize Baghdad, but were spread far too thin to halt the looting and sabotage of Iraq's "physical, economic, and institutional" infrastructure. Washington's postwar planning had been handicapped by the expectation of being greeted as liberators as well as by rivalries between the Pentagon and State Department. Even as these expectations were collapsing,

> the Bush Administration compounded its initial mistakes by stubbornly refusing to send in more troops. Administration officials repeatedly deluded themselves into believing that the defeat of the insurgency was just around the corner—just as soon as the long hot summer of 2003 ended, or reconstruction dollars started flowing in and jobs were created, or the political transition began, or Saddam Hussein was captured, or the interim government was inaugurated. As in Vietnam, a turning point always seemed imminent and Washington refused to grasp the depth of popular disaffection.[14]

It would have been impolitic for a former adviser to the Coalition Provisional Authority to have said so, but the situation was even worse than Diamond's grim article indicated. The disbanding of the Iraqi military had been a major mistake, adding to the ranks of the unemployed while providing the insurgency and various armed militias with a virtual shopping list of disaffected and trained recruits.[15] As internal conflict within Iraq worsened, its military forces would have to be reinvented, a task that had only begun when Ambassador Bremer left in June, after turning the government back to Iraqi control. Building or rebuilding any army is a long, arduous, and expensive proposition, but until those seeds began bearing fruit, American forces would have to do the job. With every month and each new casualty, the questions grew more insistent. Both kinds of interviews now typically ended with the query, "When do you think our troops will be out of there, Colonel?"

It would have been similarly impolitic of me on those occasions to have held up a picture of President Bush and replied, "I don't know. Why don't you ask him?" But after November, it was a struggle to escape the conclusion that the Bush administration had dodged a bullet. Given the enormity of what remained to be done before the United States could even think of ending its involvement in Iraq, Abu Ghraib had been at best a tactical issue. So too had been the tough, bloody fight that left the Marines in control of Fallujah, a victory that left all the Warheads moved by the courage, professionalism and heroism of our comrades in arms.[16]

Not that we were allowed to talk about those sorts of things on-air very much. Maybe on Memorial Day or Veterans Day a story might appear about a soldier receiving multiple Purple Hearts or, if it was particularly compelling, of a Marine's heroism being rewarded with a Silver Star. If contemporary correspondents were customarily fixated on providing voice-over commentaries of the latest combat disaster videos, it also meant they had largely abandoned the compelling, first-person narratives provided by Ernie Pyle and Joe Galloway in World War II and Vietnam.[17]

That narrative tradition had been an enduring journalistic counterpoint, a balance between the horror of war and its partial redemption by acts of individual heroism. Bing West was also struck by this contrast and in a widely noted opinion piece noted that in Fallujah,

> Hundreds of gripping stories of valor emerged that would have been publicized in World War II. Although there are far more heroes than louts in the ranks, stories of the abuses at Abu Ghraib…vastly outnumber stories of heroism and sacrifice….Why was valor considered front-page news in 1945 and abuse considered front-page news in 2005?…Fed a steady diet of stories about bad conduct and deprived of models of valor, the youth of America will eventually decline to serve. As the poet Pindar wrote, "Unsung, the noblest deed will die."[18]

In one sense, of course, the youth of America had already issued such a refusal—a not-so-very-polite RSVP that, as upwardly mobile future yuppies, they had better things to do than fulfilling the traditional obligation of serving in the ranks during wartime. Other than the heroes of Fallujah, Kirkuk, and Mosul, you could call even them the Not-So-Great-Generation. As humans, we find it almost impossible to be very much interested in people with whom we have little in common, and for all our guilty approbations, the Soldiers had become *them*, not us. Why else would the hyperactive media never even bother to suggest the importance, in an election year, for the American people to think very carefully about the sacrifices being made by other people's kids, sacrifices that almost certainly were just a down payment on what lay ahead. Sobering as those questions were, what if Iraq were the least of our problems now that we were being confronted by enemies who would never quit, who would simply be emboldened if we withdrew? And what if those enemies believed so deeply in jihad that they were willing to give it their all, rather than just fighting on the cheap?

Those were the toughest questions of all and we had asked none of them because that was simply not done in the Electronic Coliseum. There was never a good reason to stampede the plebeians because, with their remote controls, things could quickly turn ugly. In fact, it was possible to think of cable news as a kind of "Easy Button" that transported you instantly into the risers of the Electronic Coliseum, a place where you were not really exposed to news but rather to the *latest in nonfiction television*. If that sounds harsh, then blame it on our friends at Journalism.org and the Pew Center because the phrase is theirs. So is this final judgment:

> These trends are true at all three cable channels.... The whole picture, at all three networks, is of a medium with enormous time to fill, with a great deal of repetition and perhaps with an impression of immediacy that is greater than reality. Viewers get closer to the raw elements that once went into journalism rather than what, in other forms of television news, was once considered the end product.[19]

If journalism had long been understood as the first draft of history, then cable news had lately become the first draft of that first draft.

It may just be simpler to blame the whole thing on the senior producers and their constant need to medicate the presumed attention deficit disorders of the cable audience. Of all the Warheads, Jack Jacobs may have been the only one to strike a subtle blow for freedom and thus give them a small measure of comeuppance. On one in-studio hit, Jack was paired with Lester Holt when they were asked to do a tight side-by-side shot. Lester Holt stands over six feet tall and Jack...well...doesn't. In fact, a favorite practical joke of the bookers on a slow day is to retrieve Jack's suit coat from a hanger and shout, "Jack, is this yours or is G.I. Joe opening a pinstripe line?" The stage crew had dealt with the height differential before and quickly brought a box for Jack to stand on, perfect for the tight, waist-level shot the scene called for. Lester and Jack finished their hit together. In the far-off control room the senior producer may have missed something because he shouted imperiously to the controllers. "WRAP...BUMP SHOT...NOW!" Instantly the camera shot changed from waist to panoramic, and there stood Jack exposed to the nationwide TV audience—our very own Medal of Honor recipient standing on an orange crate. Those tapes were ordered seized and confiscated, but the MSNBC Archives Department has let it be known that, while being opposed to bribes, they are not fanatics either.

---

[1] Journalism.org, "The State of the News Media 2004: Cable TV," *Annual Report on American Journalism*, n.d., 6–7.

[2] "Democrats Lean Left and Oppose the War," *New York Times*, July 25, 2004.

[3] Peter J. Boyer, "General Clark's Battles," *The New Yorker*, November 17, 2003, p.70.

[4] Wesley K. Clark, *Winning Modern War* (New York: PublicAffairs, 2003), 159.

[5] "Please Turn Down the War, We Can't Hear the Other Issues," *New York Times*, October 3, 2004.

[6] Journalism.org, "The State of the News Media" 2004–5. Available at http://www.stateofthemedia.org/2004/narrative_cabletv and http://www.stateofthemedia.org/2005/printable_cabletv.

[7] Journalism.org 2004, op. cit., 5.

[8] Pew Research Center, "News Audience Increasingly Politicized," June 8, 2004. Available at http://people-press.org/reports/

[9] Paul Vallely and Thomas McInerny, *Endgame* (New York: Regnery, 2004), 167–68.

[10] 2004 Survey, op. cit., 1.

[11] New York, New York, Committee for the Protection of Journalists, "Iraq: Journalists in Danger." Available at http://www.cpj.org/Briefings/Iraq/Iraq_danger.html.

[12] See the sequence of reports on the prisoner abuse scandal by Robin Wright, Bradley Graham, and David von Drehle, *Washington Post*, May 6–8, 2004.

[13] James Brady, *Flyboys: A True Story of Courage* (Boston: Little Brown & Company, 2003).

[14] Larry Diamond, "What Went Wrong in Iraq," *Foreign Affairs* 83:5 (Sept/Oct, 2004), 34–56.

[15] Bremer's justification for that decision is in his memoir, *My Year in Iraq* (New York: Simon & Schuster, 2006), 54–59.

[16] The classic account of that victory is by Bing West, *No True Glory: A First-Hand Account of the Battle for Fallujah* (New York: Bantam, 2005).

[17] See, for example, the classic by Hal Moore and Joe Galloway, *We Were Soldiers Once and Young* (New York: Random House, 1992).

[18] Bing West, "Slighting this Greatest Generation," *Washington Post*, Oct. 9, 2005, B7.

[19] Journalism.org, "State of the News Media 2004," 11.

CHAPTER EIGHT

Tipping Point—Baghdad 2005

· · · · ·

F rom the glass wall of the C-130's cockpit, the Iraqi desert far below unrolled in the haze like an endless brown carpet. Splashes of vegetation traced the faint outlines of the Tigris and Euphrates river valleys, now becoming more frequent against the smog on the far horizon that cloaked Baghdad. We were an hour out of Kuwait, the deceptive calm of the flight never quite putting to rest the unsettling consciousness of flying into a war zone, the airspace we were now so easily transiting having been a zone of confrontation for more than a dozen years. Naturally, the Warheads snapped pictures, each of us cycling one by one up the ladder and into the cockpit to record this leg of the "U.S. Department of Defense Military Analyst Trip to Iraq, December 6–11, 2005."

Looking down upon the sere brown vistas of the terrain we had fought for prompted long-lost memories of a Staff College exercise in which as young majors we had been given extensive maps, studies, and surveys of an unnamed Middle Eastern country and asked for our notional recommendations. Should we, the instructors intoned imperiously, recommend to the National Command Authorities that U.S. forces *attack*, *defend*, or *do nothing* in support of American national objectives in this region? One of my classmates had given our collective answer—and a fourth option. "Sir, our seminar has analyzed the data and believes our recommendation should be: *leave 'em alone and let 'em suffer*. Nothing that U.S. forces could ever do to these people would be half as bad as what they have right now." The faculty had laughed right along with us as we promptly moved on to present the *attack* alternative: while it wasn't always the preferred Staff College solution, the *do nothing* option was normally considered the purview of the State Department. The view out the cockpit window made me ruefully wonder if our original finding had been correct after all.

Had Dick Cheney been present those thoughts would surely have been derided as isolationist or even defeatist, but it had been that kind of year. In January, all the cable networks were scrambling to cover the Asian tsunami, the worst natural disaster in modern memory and an eerie foreshadowing of Hurricane Katrina's wrath just nine months later. Yet even in the ruins of Banda Aceh, there were constant reminders of the limits of any intervention, even for the very best humanitarian reasons. Marines arriving on rescue ships had been ordered ashore without their standard weapons and armor, while Indonesian authorities made clear there would be limits imposed on the numbers and duration of foreign relief workers. Any story shifts, and in the days that followed, attention was increasingly redirected from tragedy and dire necessity toward the tsunami's survivors, particularly the animals and certain native populations, who seemed to have known something was coming. Had some sort of jungle extrasensory perception (ESP) been at work and how had it provided a warning that saved the lives of some humans and most of the animals?

Even here there were lessons for the unwary outsider because as the story shifted, the fate and whereabouts of the Andaman and Nicobar Islanders gradually took on some significance. Many of the islands, a little-known archipelago in the Bay of Bengal, were lower than the reported wave heights of the tsunami. One of our most experienced MSNBC bookers, Florence Squassi, was given a seemingly impossible task. She was directed to (a) find someone with strong professional credentials who actually knew where these islands were; (b) was able to say something sensible about them; and (c) do that on TV, which meant taking less than three minutes precisely when cued to do so. How she did all that remains a closely held trade secret, but in hours Florence had unearthed Dr. Bennett Bronson, a curator of Chicago's Field Museum, an expert in Asian anthropology, and an authority on the Andaman Islanders.

In due course, he appeared in the studios of our Chicago affiliate. There is no hard-and-fast guide to these things, but with his waxed mustache, blazer, and designer tie, Dr. Bronson somehow looked every inch the part of a distinguished anthropologist. He lost very little time debunking the idea that ESP might have been at work: however primitive by Western standards, these people were closely attuned to their environment. The survival lessons accumulated over eons had taught them one basic truth: that when the birds, monkeys, and elephants suddenly took off for high ground, this was also a sensible course of action for any adjacent humans even slightly interested in self-preservation. Did we have any idea how many of the Andaman Islanders had survived? As our anchor framed that question, the studio monitor showed the corners of Dr. Bronson's mustache turning up even higher. Not really, he replied, *because an Indian navy launch approaching the shore had been greeted by a volley of arrows.* Shortly thereafter an Indian navy helicopter attempting to land on the island had been greeted in the same rude way, but now the volley of arrows was even more intense. In short Dr. Bronson concluded, "I simply think we need to respect the wishes of the Andaman Islanders to be left alone."

From my hidden corner in the booker's nook of the studio, I let out a roar of approval and gave Florence a high-five for her efforts in nailing such an interesting guest. What might have been intended as a "feel good" story really hadn't been that at all; but as a demonstration of human persistence and sheer cussedness against tsunamis, outsiders, and all other comers, this one was hard to beat. Dr. Bronson was invited back for a repeat performance the next day. "Didja notice that he wore a pullover sweater the second time?" the irrepressible Florence observed. "Didn't take him long to figure out our deal, hanh?" By now there was even a picture snapped from that Indian helicopter—probably in some haste—of a mean-looking Andaman Islander with a quite respectable longbow that he was aiming slightly high and to the left. The photograph was grainy enough that it was difficult to tell, but it seemed that at least one of his fingers was upturned in what anthropologists like Dr. Bronson would surely tell us is the universal symbol among the Andaman Islanders for good luck.

Something very much like that appeared to be going on in Iraq as well. One of the more consistently reliable sources of information on the insurgency was provided by Anthony H. Cordesman, a former Georgetown faculty colleague and holder of the Arleigh A. Burke Chairman of Strategy at Washington's Center for Strategic and International Studies (CSIS). On the CSIS Web site, Tony was reporting that the insurgency persisted, that attacks widely fluctuated, that they were concentrated in only four of Iraq's eighteen provinces, but that the 42 percent of the Iraqi population living in those four provinces accounted for 85 percent of the violence. With Iraqi elections taking place throughout 2005, the insurgents had broadened their targets to political assassinations, kidnapping foreigners, and attacking the already fragile Iraqi infrastructure. Most unsettling was Cordesman's finding that the insurgency was being prosecuted by the equivalent of a "distributed network" of well-organized cells but lacking the traditional military hierarchy or other top-down structures. This structure—or rather nonstructure—allowed the insurgents to use "low-technology swarm tactics" against targets of opportunity suggested by open sources and the effective use of Internet-based intelligence:

> The ability to "swarm" against vulnerable civil and military targets at the time of the insurgent's choosing, and to focus on political and

media effects sharply reduces the need to fight battles—particularly if the odds are against the insurgents.[1]

In short, the theoretical fight between hierarchies and networks—predicted by Arquilla and Ronfeldt and regularly injected into the minds of my Georgetown students for most of a decade—had come fully alive and was now being played out in deadly earnest in the struggle for Iraq.[2]

A slightly more upbeat midyear assessment had been offered by Gen. Barry Mc-Caffrey to the Senate Foreign Relations Committee, the result of a weeklong fact-finding trip to Iraq. It had been a short but intense trip because his sources were impeccable: more than thirty meetings with every level of the U.S. and Iraqi chains of command. His assessment: "U.S. Military forces in Iraq are superb.... Unit effectiveness is as good as we can get. This is the most competent and battle-wise force in our nation's history." However, the Iraq insurgency was also "more complex than Vietnam" and the next six months (i.e., July–December 2005) would be a crucial turning point in the war. If political progress continued and the Iraqi security forces were rebuilt into a ten-division, 250,000-strong force, "the energy will start draining out of the insurgency" and U.S. troops might begin withdrawing by late summer 2006. He warned the Senate as well about the dangers of a premature withdrawal and left his readers with this brutally candid assessment: "We must continue to level with the American people. We still have a five-year fight facing us in Iraq."[3]

On one thing, though, Cordesman and McCaffrey both agreed: that there was an ever-present chance of civil war in Iraq, either through political ineptitude, successful insurgent campaigns, or some combination of both. Because war was even more complex than the "Pottery Barn" comment often attributed to Colin Powell during the run-up to Iraq—that if you break it, you pay for it. Clausewitz, Machiavelli, and even Sun Tzu had warned across several millennia that all war is chance, that there is something indefinable and unpredictable about unleashing its forces, and that the Pottery Barn metaphor might be appropriate only if they sold Pandora's Box. Those forces were clearly now at work in Iraq, and the United States had made some fundamental mistakes that were becoming familiar. As Barry's report had put it, our intervention had taken down "a criminal regime and left a nation without an operational state"; but then the "transitional Bremer-appointed Iraqi government created a weak state of warring factions."[4]

The Rumsfeld crowd had never understood that it might take more troops to win the peace than to take down the regime, apparently having missed the point that the classic function of any defense ministry in a nation at war is "force generation"—raising enough forces to prevail. Not only were there no more American forces available to send beyond the 130,000 already there, but also its designated viceroy had simply disbanded what was left of the existing Iraqi army, so there was no one else to turn things over to when we wanted to leave. Worst of all, we had wasted precious time, possibly twelve to fifteen months. It had taken us that long to recognize not only the scope of the insurgency, but also that the key to its defeat and an eventual American exit were one and the same: the re-creation of a competent Iraqi security force. Time in warfare is the one element you share with the enemy and the insurgents had used their portion to organize a persistent strategy that was having its intended effect not only upon American soldiers but also on the political will of the nation that had sent them. Roughly seventy of our soldiers were dying in Iraq each month, and while they were surely "other peoples' kids," the nation was growing tired of it. The weekend before we left Washington for Iraq, the papers and talk shows had still been swirling with the controversy kicked off the month before when Congressman Jack Murtha, one of the few veterans on Capitol Hill, called for the immediate withdrawal of an American force that was already being described by some as "broken."[5]

It was a lot to think about, and while Barry McCaffrey had been lavished with a week's worth of attention and interviews, the other Warheads on this trip would have to gain such impressions as we might in the space of just three days. Our time would be short, so it was somewhat comforting to recall how my dissertation adviser had been granted a rare visa when Red China had first cracked open its gates to Western academics. His visa had been good for just three days back then too, but on his return he had starred in a lecture series ingeniously entitled, "China: Yesterday, Today, and Tomorrow." Our "tactical landing" in Baghdad and movement by helicopter to the Green Zone was a useful introduction to the fast, furtive, and fully armed operations characterizing the U.S. contingent in Iraq. Having flown in Army helicopters almost every day in Bosnia, I easily recognized the high-speed, low-altitude, tight turns and taut flaring on every landing as subtle signs that this was an altogether different kind of engagement. The alert waist gunners and the comforting presence of Apache gunships on our flank and "6" positions were additional signs, but not subtle at all.

There was no way to know in advance, but our brief visit would provide some important clues about the American effort in Iraq, clues that would be gradually fleshed out after I returned to the United States. We were indeed at the tipping point, with the eventual outcome uncertain. But that Americans were still in the game—especially after having made so many basic mistakes early on—was due to three critical factors:

1. *Extraordinary leadership in the field:* Ultimately the responsibility for everything the American contingent did would rest upon the shoulders of Gen. George Casey, its overall commander. But the key to the entire effort would be the re-building of the Iraqi security forces, and here Lt. Gen. David Petraeus had made an extraordinary contribution.

2. *Exploitation and application of an advanced technology:* Where every other factor in the theater of operations worked against them, the exploitation of geospatial intelligence by the American contingent—although little understood or appreci-ated outside military channels—represented an unheralded advance that partially offset the "home field advantage" enjoyed by the insurgents. The hero here was retired Air Force Lt. Gen. Jim Clapper, director of the National Geospatial Intelligence Agency.

3. *Tactical adaptation to counterinsurgency warfare:* Geospatial intelligence or any other tactical information has very little meaning unless it can be provided to the warrior on the ground—easily, routinely, and in time to make a difference. Army Lt. Gen. J. R. Vines, the ground component's tactical commander in Iraq, took the extraordinary step of engineering a system—FUSION NET—which did precisely that. The result was more effective information sharing at the lowest tactical lev-els, but even this was merely a way point in the Army's rapid adaptation to the demands of counterinsurgency warfare.

Building the new Iraqi security force

General Petraeus was an old friend from West Point faculty days with whom I had been in regular contact on both sides of his back-to-back deployments to Iraq—beginning with command of the 101st Airborne Division in the assault on Baghdad, efforts profiled in Rick Atkinson's book, *In the Company of Soldiers.*[6] It took the Pentagon-directed presence of the embeds to get a Pulitzer Prize–winning author like Atkinson so close to Petraeus, who well understood that publicity is to a rising military career what cholesterol is to the human circula-tory system. As a friend of twenty years standing, I was presumably numbered as "good" cholesterol, but knew not to push my luck. When Dave was ordered back to Iraq after the return of Ambassador Paul Bremer in May 2004, and placed in charge of the effort to rebuild the Iraqi army, one could only e-mail him best wishes and secretly hope it was not a setup. The reason? The only thing tougher than constructing an army is doing so when the nation in question is in the midst of a civil war—part of the reason why Lincoln had been so pleased with his discovery of Grant.

Petraeus had been handed one of the toughest assignments the Pentagon can give, assuming his new responsibilities under distressingly chaotic conditions. Bremer had presided over an underresourced ad hockery that simply threw piecemeal such Iraqi forces as could be quickly gathered together into cauldrons like Fallujah and elsewhere, where their failure had not been left to chance.[7] Bremer was replaced by Ambassador John Negroponte, who promptly reallocated almost $2 billion in reconstruction funds for the rebuilding of the security forces—subsequently increased to $5 billion. The new funds were only a down payment on what would eventually be needed, but they permitted the first real modernization the Iraqis had seen since the end of the war and the delivery of some of the basics—uniforms, weapons, trucks, and radios. Equally significant was the personal involvement of Defense Secretary Rumsfeld who, following this second "regime change" in Baghdad, became far more active in stimulating a comprehensive view of what the new Iraqi security force should look like, at national, regional, and local levels. By the end of 2004, a blueprint had been drawn up calling for the creation of up to ten Iraqi divisions, organized into 140 combat battalions and, within two years, comprising a quarter of a million soldiers.

General Casey joined in the effort, but Petraeus had organized most of the planning with a handpicked staff that day-to-day averaged less than a dozen officers. While the group involved came to grips with the hard questions of "right-sizing" the new Iraqi force and then justifying their recommendations to congressional budgeters, Petraeus increasingly turned his attention over the winter of 2004–05 to other matters. It had been one thing to sweep away the old Iraqi military structure, but nothing had been done to re-create the key infrastructures on which any modern army depends. Logistical structures needed to be put in place, beginning with an organized system of depots to store equipment and spare parts; indeed a coherent system for organizing and inventory first needed to be invented. Maintenance, maintenance procedures, maintenance facilities, and maintenance personnel either did not exist or were in rudimentary condition. The elements of an organized personnel system from basic skill levels to retention and promotion policies reflected either the ancien regime or no regime whatsoever.

While the new Iraqi army would need to reinvent itself in order to become a bastion of national unity, it was ironic that there was no real system of professional military education as most Western armies would today understand that term. Petraeus began to plan the painstaking reestablishment of educational institutions for Iraqi officers, noncommissioned officers, and soldiers. These schools would teach the military skills that had atrophied under Saddam as well as venturing into the previously unknown world of ethics, inculcating basic precepts of fairness where privilege, ethnicity, and simple survival skills had long held sway. Leadership would be studied at a new military academy and at staff colleges. It was an ambitious agenda, yet these were fundamental tasks if an Iraqi army was to be built on the ruins left by Saddam, who had not only left a shambles but a lingering legacy of suspicion and distrust. "The Iraqi military really wasn't organized as a team the way we are," one of the planners of the first Gulf War had told my classes at Georgetown. "They were more like a mafia conspiracy." In the institutions Petraeus was now rebuilding, that institutional history had to be steadily overcome.

By June 2005, Barry McCaffrey would note in his report that the hastily drawn blue-prints for their reconstruction as well as the steady injection of American funding now made the Iraqi security forces a "real and hugely significant factor. Gen. Dave Petraeus has done a brilliant job with his supporting trainers." Already 169,000 of the Army and police were in the field—some in combat—equipped with "uniforms, automatic weapons, [and] body armor" as well as light trucks, tanks, and communications gear. But while these forces were steadily growing in effectiveness, the record was mixed: insurgents were widely believed to have infiltrated the ranks, and logistics as well as command and control remained problematic. And more ominously, "Corruption is a…greater long-range danger than the armed insurgency."[8]

As proof that in Washington no good deed goes unpunished, the steady progress in developing the Iraqi security forces nevertheless generated its own heat when, at the end of September, Gen. George Casey was embroiled in a meaningless controversy during a hearing of the Senate Armed Services Committee. How many Iraqi battalions were now at the highest readiness level, the senators wanted to know. Wasn't it true that the numbers had recently gone from three to one, and wasn't this proof that our training program had not made the progress that had been hoped for? George did well to hold his temper and to refrain from observing that the readiness figures for an army hastily reconstructed in the midst of civil war could only be benchmarks—with the same tentative meaning as "The Honorable" offsetting the name of each member of Congress.

But the Warheads would receive the benefit of one of the not-so-easily quantified investments that Petraeus had helped arrange: a visit to the new Iraqi Military Academy at Al Rustimayah, southeast of Baghdad. The helicopters had bobbed and weaved over urban terrain and farmlands before flaring into a landing zone on the edge of a village that was nonchalantly burning its weekend trash. But what made this arrival especially memorable was that it was punctuated with the unmistakable crack of AK-47 rifle fire as the cadets went through their tactical exercises. They were undergoing a regime that would have done credit to any military school: obstacle and confidence courses, combat first aid, physical training, ambush techniques, and even an exercise (complete with automatic weapons and smoke grenades) recognizable as "rifle platoon in the attack." Assembled on the parade ground, the graduating class was smartly practicing drill and ceremonies, husbanded at every step by a regimental sergeant major from the Coldstream Guards. The commandant was a British army colonel, who gestured at his charges and said proudly, "They would drill like this all day if we would let them. It's part of their cul-CHAH." It was my first up-close-and-personal look at the new Iraqi soldier: lean, brown, tough little bastards. I also remember thinking that the Brit was right about the Iraqi culture too, because it went back 2,700 years—to Sargon, Sennacherib, and those Assyrian horse archers you read about in the Old Testament.

Their ancient and modern heritage had instilled an iron discipline that held even in the hot sun as Eric Ruff, an assistant to Donald Rumsfeld, and Tom McInerny succumbed to the usual temptation to say a few words. We had been warned several times to avoid taking pictures of anyone's faces because the insurgents routinely targeted the cadets, their instructors, and even their families. But when those young Iraqi soldiers got a close look at Air Force Capt. Nicole Barnum, all bets were off. It took them roughly five seconds to decide that, speeches aside, the Americans must not be all bad if they were bringing such attractive women to Iraq, and could they please have their pictures taken with her? To stave off a riot, we obliged, snapped away, stayed for lunch, tested the limits of the interpreter's patience, and for the first time looked into the eyes of the new Iraq, because these young soldiers were clearly the ones with the real skin in the game and the ones who would lose the most if the insurgents succeeded.

When I got back, Dave Petraeus and I finally caught up with each other over the phone. He was curious about Al Rustimayah and pensive about the challenges its first graduates were facing at that moment as Iraq tottered on the brink of civil war. He was now commanding the Army's Combined Arms Center at Fort Leavenworth and helping to acquaint the Army's future leaders with the lessons that had been learned in places like Iraq and Afghanistan. He referred me to an article then headlining *Military Review*, the Army's premiere tactical journal. There Petraeus had approvingly quoted T. E. Lawrence—Lawrence of Arabia—in words written during World War I: "Do not try to do too much with your own hands....Better the Arabs do it tolerably than that you do it perfectly. It is their war and you are to help them, not win it for them....It may take them longer and it may not be as good as you think, but if it theirs, it will be better."

Having bridged both cultures, Petraeus was able to articulate in gentle terms an important lesson for the hard-charging, "can do," action-oriented American soldier. Empowering Iraqis was essential in rebuilding their infrastructure, re-creating their army, or conducting counterinsurgency operations. In fact, "empowering, enabling and assisting the Iraqis" was now a fundamental part of American strategy.[9] The subtext was, traditional leadership skills would surely have to adapt as the Army prepared to fight the counterinsurgency wars of the twenty-first century.

Exploiting geospatial intelligence

The jet lag from our twenty-four-hour journey across eight time zones had by now fully kicked in, we had enjoyed a heavy lunch with U.S. Ambassador Zalmay Khalilzad and were now deep in the Green Zone seated in a cramped conference room in one of Saddam's former palaces. The architectural style was early Mussolini, the toilets leaked even though some were made from marble, and the whole place was suffused with an atmosphere in which "tacky" would have represented a distinct improvement. We were, of course, sitting through the usual barrage of PowerPoint briefings that were as instinctive to the Army as Kevlar and MREs. I was mentally composing a future op-ed, "Should PowerPoints Be Made a Court-Martial Offense?" when the two-star heading coalition intelligence operations took the podium. He presented a surprisingly upbeat picture of how tactical intelligence was working against the insurgency; it was eye-opening but it also awakened my skepticism. Networks are tough things to penetrate, especially for a technology-suffused force such as the U.S. Army, where intelligence officers were far more likely to launch off into discussions of gateways, baud rates, and gigabits than to know anything interesting about an actual *enemy*.

In Bosnia, there was little useful human intelligence (HUMINT) developed against the Serbs, who followed the old-style Soviet approach and simply avoided yammering on phones or radios. As a result, we were often surprised by the routine, although the PowerPoints were usually first rate. In an insurgency, however, HUMINT is the coin of the realm. "General, at what point did the HUMINT get better?" I asked. He paused and carefully replied that with the rebuilding of the Iraqi Army, we now had an effective partner in the systematic gathering of HUMINT, because Arab armies fully understood its importance. He paused and then made a startling statement: "But the biggest single improvement in our operations has been the way we have been able to use geospatial intelligence." The Warhead sitting next to me now whispered urgently, "Whut in the *hayull* is ge-yo-*special* intelligence?" "Relax. It's something that you will never ever see on MSNBC or any other network," I replied reassuringly.

The fact was that I actually knew something about it, not through my Warhead or network affiliations, but because I had given a speech just a month before in San Antonio to a working convention of the National Geospatial-Intelligence

Agency (NGA). The invitation had come from an old friend, Jim Clapper, a retired Air Force lieutenant general, who had taken over as NGA director the day after 9-11. Jim is something of a legend, a brilliant, gregarious, anarchist in uniform whose people just adored him. In San Antonio he had attended receptions on the city's famous Riverwalk attired in jeans and sporting an enormous foam rubber cowboy hat that marked his passage from blocks away. While other people talked about transformation, Jim had quietly presided over a revolution that not many in Washington or elsewhere ever bothered to notice.

At the simplest level, geospatial intelligence (GEOINT) was the offspring of the digital and video revolutions—both driven by commercial rather than governmental needs. Its components were imagery—pictures of all kinds supplied by platforms ranging from the earth's surface all the way to outer space; imagery intelligence—the correlation of those pictures with database information; and geospatial information—the precise measurement of objects and their common reference to the earth's surface. In Operation Desert Storm, the GPS had made its debut—and instantly revolutionized navigation on and off the battlefield. At first it seemed that this revolution had simply continued and that the same kinds of moving, digitized maps increasingly available as automotive options were now in the hands of the warrior. And in a sense they were, which was itself a major step forward. As recently as Grenada, war stories had persisted about Michelin guides or other tourist maps being hurriedly passed out whenever any contingency operation arose. If by some miracle of planning standard 1:50,000 tactical map sheets of the area of operations actually *were* available, it was an article of faith that any battle would be fought at the precise intersection where four of those large and ungainly charts came together. A fellow intelligence officer later swore he had received his Army Achievement Medal as a direct result of pulling out a roll of scotch tape in the middle of an exercise, thus allowing tactical operations to proceed smoothly.

But now the linkage of these underlying digital and imagery technologies had created a synergy that was fast becoming far more than the sum of its parts. Whereas before, whole fleets of cargo aircraft were needed just to transport operations maps; during the invasion of Iraq in 2003, NGA analysts simply downloaded their entire Iraqi database on hard drives and delivered them directly to units throughout the theater.[10] During the battles for Fallujah in 2004, NGA "Reachback" teams provided the Marines with high-resolution terrain data that increased the effectiveness of sniper teams, guided movement through densely packed urban terrain, and limited collateral damage while providing photographic maps that helped debunk the more outlandish claims of insurgent propaganda. Best of all, the high-resolution mapping allowed the Marines to engage in a classic ruse de guerre, conducting weeks of small attacks on the city's southern and eastern edges, before mounting the main attack from the north in a sudden charge of tightly packed formations across a preplanned front three miles wide.[11]

The ability to perform precise measurements was also bringing terrain knowledge to previously unknown levels. On an eleven-day Space Shuttle Radar Topography Mission in 2000, "synthetic aperture" radar was used to take elevation readings of approximately 80 percent of the earth's surface. It took years to process, but the data was digested in time to allow its use in Iraq, where the measurements proved sufficiently accurate that helicopter landing zones could be surveyed in advance, including whether any slopes within the zone had inclines steep enough to interfere with the rotor blades. Yet even these advantages represented only the first wave of the new digital capabilities, because the precise geolocation also allowed the integration of imagery, mapping, and intelligence data previously held separately. The overall effects of this "wedding cake" of layered information are:

> Customers who would have [previously] asked for a 1:25,000 scale map of a city now understand that they can request and receive a digital fly-through of the same city, complete with annotated ingress/egress routes in a three-dimensional format.[12]

Another clue to the effect that geospatial intelligence was having on the American contingent could be seen on the screens and white boards in the tactical operations centers at division headquarters. In Bosnia ten years before, the Predator UAV had made its operational debut, but there was only one of them usually available. Air Force authorities became cranky if operational needs suddenly developed and we asked to move it away from its agreed orbits and loiter times. Not so now: the watch officers in Baghdad confronted a bank of screens not unlike those in the control room at MSNBC, the real-time video down-linked from fleets of drones—as many as twenty at any given time—and even aerostatic blimps mixing with the feed from camera points fixed at strategic locations across the city. The technique was now called "persistent surveillance," and it was providing American commanders with the proverbial "God's-eye view" of their operational area. Aerial views of the battlefield had, of course, been part of the American tactical repertoire since the Civil War, but these were not only more persistent but infinitely more precise than anything seen before.

What was even better was that the information was digitized and standardized, meaning that it could be easily converted into map data, so that the persistent surveillance might yield permanent results. Many sacrosanct beliefs and service traditions were changing under the dusty boots of the American contingent in Iraq, although few of those things would ever be noticed by the media, electronic or otherwise. For example: Just off the Main Rotunda of the National War College in Washington hangs an impressive photo montage of the earth's surface, a Mercator projection taken over time so as to appear totally without clouds. "Looks like our idea of the perfect war, sir," one of my Air Force students had pointed out, and for a long time I schemed to substitute his quip for the caption chosen by the class who had donated it: EVERYTHING CHANGES EXCEPT THE GEOGRAPHY. It might have been better had my covert campaign succeeded because the Asian tsunami and Hurricane Katrina, as well as the urban combat in Iraq and the mountain warfare in Afghanistan, were demonstrating how the geography was constantly changing. It had been the genius of Jim Clapper and his NGA colleagues to recognize that fact, to invent a whole new intelligence discipline to deal with it, and then to convince the Pentagon to let them try it out in war's ultimate proving ground. That martial tradition includes great captains like Napoleon who used advances in cartography to plot his strategies of conquest, or "war upon the map" as he termed it. But for the American warriors in Iraq the matter was much more straightforward: in a situation where every other factor conspired to give the insurgent home field advantage, the exploitation of geospatial intelligence had helped to level the playing field.

Tactical adaptation to counterinsurgency warfare

We were having dinner with General Casey at his quarters in Baghdad, commandeered after having served as another of Saddam's mini palaces. The garish tapestries and ornate terra-cotta bird bath lamps were a triumph of bad taste, as if the Beverly Hillbillies had been Shriners. On arriving I had hugged the general and said, "Hi, George. Love what you've done with the place." The years fell away in an instant and the Warheads became just another group of old comrades in arms sharing stories, insights, and jokes. As it usually did in these circumstances the volume level increased. Now Casey was teasing his ground force commander, Lt. Gen. J. R. Vines, about the latest task he had inherited over lunch the day before. "Sir, that wasn't my fault," Vines replied quickly. "It's just that those MRE packets only come with plastic knives and they weren't quite strong enough to let me slash my wrists before having to accept the mission." We all laughed and thus received our introduction to "J.R."—the man Barry McCaffrey had called "the most experienced and effective operational battle leader we have produced in a generation."[13]

We met up again with General Vines the next day in, naturally, another of Saddam's palaces, this one dedicated to the memory of the Iraqi "victory" over Iran in the 1980s, in reality a long, pointless, and particularly bloody struggle. There was an interesting picture above Vines's desk—a large, color photograph of the Twin Towers burning on 9-11. "Helps to keep me focused," he replied when asked about it. We followed up on the previous day's discussion, and while he agreed that geospatial intelligence was essential, Vines reinforced the overriding importance of human intelligence in everything they did. Even his brigade commanders were expected to run their own sources and to develop their own information rather than having it spoon fed down the magic data pipeline from on high. Combat information needed to be developed locally, followed up promptly, and acted upon instantaneously if it had any chance of yielding significant results; if it didn't, then it was history, interesting but essentially useless. The reason is that the enemy was a network, not a Soviet hierarchy even more slow-moving than we were. The key to defeating it was to roll up that network in the same way that a doctor fights cancer: one cell at a time. "How well is that going, General?" someone asked. Vines had an aide pull out a large chart showing names and bearded faces, many of which had been crossed out. "Remember that old whack-a-mole game you used to play back at the county fair, son?" he replied quietly.

This was astounding. There had been a time in the not-so-very-distant past in which line officers had considered intelligence as theoretically important but something you usually obtained only after taking the hill and counting the bodies. The first Gulf War had changed most of that, but the adjustment General Vines was talking about—from fighting main force units to a network-centered counterinsurgency—was every bit as significant. But something was still missing. "General, you're going after networks but you're still a hierarchy. How do you share such perishable information in a top-down Army?" I asked. He smiled again. "FUSION NET. It's an open-source system we set up here in Iraq, based on what I used in Afghanistan. We knew we needed to bring a lot of systems together, cross a lot of boundaries, and make it quick and easy." There were few opportunities to question him at length, but General Vines offered several follow-up sessions after he and his staff returned to the United States at the end of their tour in Iraq only a few weeks later.

From those conversations a stunning picture emerged. Even before deploying, Vines had sketched out to his communications and intelligence officers the kind of tactical information-sharing network he wanted, telling them to get started pronto. With his help, they cut procurement red tape, used only in-country contractor assistance, and in roughly eight months had a functioning system, all at the relatively modest cost of less than $10 million. Because the system was unclassified, it simply "piggybacked" atop existing communications pathways and could be used anywhere. Since it was based on existing commercial products, the troops found it easy and convenient. Even better was that because it had been developed in-house, the government now owned the software, freeing FUSION NET from the tyrannies of program managers, predatory contractors, and their proprietary software.

Yet these were only the technicalities. Like geospatial intelligence, the most valuable thing about this out-of-wedlock new system may have been that it provided a common frame of reference for widely varying activities and data points. General Vines imposed only one rule: *the authorization to move meant the requirement to report.* A convoy moving from Baghdad to Fallujah, for example, would query the system for the most current information on the area they would be passing through, including ambushes, IEDs, or any other problems noted on the route of march by any other unit. On their return, they would contribute their own observations into the system—an electronic filing that usually took less than five minutes. Route reports, after-action reviews, maps, and even videos were easily accommodated by the system, and it became a tactical library no farther away than the nearest laptop.

As with many small beginnings, FUSION NET camouflaged a major difference in philosophy. Systematic data collection and the shared common reference meant that enemy patterns could be analyzed, understood, and exploited. If IEDs were being reported in an area, for example, more attention might be directed there. When another device was found, it might not be immediately disarmed but instead placed under "persistent surveillance" until an insurgent team came to adjust the IED or move its location. When they did, the hawk would strike, teams moving in to kill or capture the insurgent cell, questioning anyone caught, and then immediately exploiting the intelligence thus gained. Pattern analysis is a standard tool of counterintelligence and police work, yet it represented a profound if subtle mental adjustment: threats were seen as symptoms to be subjected to the full range of prophylactic measures. Similarly commanders at every level could now have access to raw information for decision and exploitation, rather than having it massaged into PowerPoints. Command briefings were no longer the preferred destination of tactical information; now the target was the decision cycle of insurgent commanders.

The more I talked with General Vines and his staff, the more it seemed as if I had seen something like this before. Earlier in the year Lester Holt had been our afternoon anchor when I got word that some interesting new video had arrived. I watched it several times before going on-air as Lester's anchor buddy to narrate the sequence. What appeared to be gun-camera footage from an aircraft showed two things: the explosive detonation of a roadside IED quickly followed by the fast exit of the insurgent trigger team as they escaped the area by car. The camera smoothly tracked the car as it turned this way and that, finally halting inside the walled courtyard of a farm complex where shadowy figures could be seen entering the adjacent buildings. An instant later the camera panned back to a wider view, where American helicopters could be seen landing in an adjacent field, where troops rapidly dismounted and headed toward the farm, firing as they went. Explosions could be seen, but the video ended when some of the shadowy figures ran out of the building but suddenly stopped moving. "Cool video," said the senior producer, so we did the sequence three more times that afternoon.

It reminded me of a sequence from the Tom Clancy movie *Patriot Games*, only this action had not been filmed from space and was not the work of a gifted fiction writer. It seemed at the time as if the action had resulted from happenstance—that a particularly alert pilot had kept his eyes on the target and simply called in the cavalry. Now I knew better, but suspected even more. The aircraft had almost certainly been one of those unmanned aerial vehicles (UAVs), probably on a high-altitude stakeout of a known IED location—most likely the result of FUSION NET correlations. When the device went off, the explosion also triggered the start of a well-planned ambush of the insurgents by U.S. forces, the infantry ready and waiting in the helicopters, which would have been guided to the insurgent location by the eyes of the UAV. After that: the tactical proficiency of the American forces would have been expected to do the job.

Like Jim Clapper, General Vines helped put in place an innovative system that allowed such innovations to take place. It was all part of an aggressive adaptation to counterinsurgency warfare that simply seized upon FUSION NET or any other system as a tool in that process. This adaptation not only required that intelligence should drive operations but also that national and tactical intelligence organizations work together more effectively than ever before. Vines's staff described a typical sequence for operations in the Mosul area—north of Baghdad—in which special operations forces worked with tactical intelligence teams, UAVs, and infantry units to break up an insurgent cell that had been using vehicle-borne IEDs to target American personnel. Total time from the first intelligence lead to the time the American Stryker vehicles surrounded the insurgent's safe house was less than twelve hours.

By sheer coincidence, at that moment one of my former West Point cadets had been leading an infantry battalion under General Vines's overall command, but, of course, many layers deeper. A combination of luck and sheer persistence brought us together and provided a brief glimpse of life at the tactical level that clarified the headquarters' perspective the Warheads had been absorbing one PowerPoint at a time. If anything, David Petraeus's suggestion—that counterinsurgency warfare in Iraq and elsewhere would demand new skills from future Army leaders—was probably an understatement. Because what "Pete" told me about the actual combat operations of an infantry battalion fighting a highly networked insurgency sounded a lot like the classic modus operandi (MO) of an intelligence organization during the Cold War, except far deadlier.[14] The Army had always assumed that this rarified world had little to do with day-to-day tactical matters—and an important part of its post-Vietnam reforms had been the parity gradually established between the intelligence and operations officers; they were now expected to integrate their respective disciplines to better support their commanders. It seemed, however, that the evolution had not stopped there because Pete—the straight-leg, strait-laced infantry battalion commander—had morphed into his own intelligence officer.

He ran his own sources and developed his own local information resources. He had even reassigned two dozen of his soldiers to the task of intelligence analysis, where they regularly went along on raids to bring the analysis even closer to tactical realities. Intelligence they were developing on the insurgency was not merely a nice-to-have kind of thing, it was the life's blood of the unit's mission. It also determined everything else: "when we go to bed, when we get up, when we eat, and when we hit the latrine. It's what we fight for."

And they were surely in a fight, typically conducting thirty combat patrols each day that could end in shoot-outs or finger-in-the-eye, knee-in-the-groin fistfights with insurgent cells. Pete had already been wounded once—that's why he was in Baghdad now—and constantly recognized the bravery of his troops with medals and every kind of citation. HUMINT was the coin of this new realm and teams of special agents and interrogators went on each mission, using every IED and insurgent attack to recruit new informants. When their sources gave them a lead, it was instantly followed up and compared against information supplied by other sources, almost all locally developed. If it checked out, the battalion would launch an operation, typically supported by Hunter-class UAVs. Such raids tried to achieve "cascading effects," using one detainee to compromise another until an entire insurgent cell had been eliminated. Speed was essential in combating the network: "If you wait until sunup, Omar has already told Ibrahim what just happened. These people aren't stupid."

We left General Vines's headquarters and headed directly for the airport, leaving Baghdad by convoy over what had been until recently the most dangerous road in the world. Its legendary lethality had finally become a political embarrassment and an American infantry unit had been sent to secure it the good old-fashioned way: with troops, aggressive patrolling, and the systematic elimination of potential ambush points. The ride was now pleasantly uneventful, our guards alert but relaxed with their CAR-14 carbines on Safe. Although tired, I was pumped up. Things still seemed to be at a tipping point, but the troops I had seen were professional, confident, and lethal, in no way a broken force. Just the opposite was true: the soldiers thought they were winning and usually found a way to chide me by asking why the media was not reporting the same war they were fighting every day.

The United States had put those soldiers at an enormous disadvantage by not ensuring enough of them were present, by not designing an effective postwar strategy, and above all by wasting time. Napoleon had written, "Strategy is the art of making use of time and space. I am less concerned about the latter than the former. Space we can recover, lost time never." Our mistakes had been fundamental, unforced errors, but American military history had often seen great leaders stepping up in just such circumstances and turning things around when all else seemed hopeless. Maybe that had been the case here, with Petraeus and the swift rebuilding of the Iraqi security forces, Clapper and the timely refining of geospatial intelligence, and Vines with his role in the Army's adaptation to counterinsurgency warfare. The tipping point was this: whether such innovations could be handed over to the Iraqis and whether they would be able to do as Lawrence of Arabia had suggested ninety years before and make them their own.

In the end much also depended on the American soldier and the nation that had sent him. I was still pondering that dilemma as our convoy dropped us by the side of the C-130 aircraft taking us back to Kuwait. The aircraft commander, an Air Force lieutenant colonel, seemed oddly subdued as he welcomed us. "Gentlemen, glad you had a good visit with our troops and that you got back here safely. I have to inform you, though, that it will be our sad duty this evening to bring two of our guys back with us." An instant hush stilled the Warheads because we knew immediately what he meant; we silently stowed our gear and strapped ourselves in. In the rear compartment of the C-130, cordoned off and bathed in soft floodlights, were two flag-draped coffins. We all knew the protocol. The flight lasted an hour, the only conversation coming in a few quickly whispered snippets. When we landed, the first duty of the aircraft and its crew was taking care of the soldiers under those flags. The ramp came down; an honor guard and a tactical ambulance were already waiting. One of us had whispered briefly to the aircraft commander and as he moved his crew down the sides of the ramp, he turned to us. "Gentlemen, if you would care to join us in rendering final honors, please do so at this time." Without a sound, we formed a neat rank on the tarmac as the coffins were prepared to leave the aircraft. The honor guard bent to their task and smoothly recovered, hands reaching out to grasp the gun-metal gray handles peeking out from under the flags. They faced front and their commander ordered "Forward March." All of us had been here many times before. Now the hairs were grayer, the steps not quite so sure, the memories possibly not as sharp but far more poignant. There are only a few occasions when old soldiers are granted the privilege of obeying the command "Present Arms." But that night, ten razor-sharp salutes snapped up smartly as our comrades in arms began their final journeys home—those "other people's kids" now being gently ushered into the Mansions of the Lord.

---

[1] Anthony A. Cordesman, eventually published as a CSIS report, *Iraq's Evolving Insurgency* (Washington, DC: CSIS, 2006), ii–iv.

[2] John Arquilla and David Ronfeldt, *The Advent of Netwar* (Santa Monica, CA: RAND, 1996). Oddly enough, this pioneering study was paid for by the Office of the Secretary of Defense during the Clinton administration, but never apparently read or applied by its successors.

[3] General Barry R. McCaffery, USA (Ret.), "Memorandum to the Senate Foreign Relations Committee: Trip Report—Kuwait and Iraq, 4 June through 11 June 2005," dated July 18, 2005. Hereafter, McCaffrey Report.

[4] Ibid., 2–3. See also on this issue the provocative critique by James Fallows, "Why Iraq Has No Army," *The Atlantic* 296:5 (December 2005): 60–77. Fallows concludes: "America's hopes today for an orderly exit from Iraq depend completely on the emergence of a viable Iraqi security force. There is no indication that such a force is about to emerge" (77).

[5] See Charles Babington, "Hawkish Democrat Joins Call for Pullout," *Washington Post*, November 18, 2005.

[6] Rick Atkinson, *In the Company of Soldiers* (New York: Henry Holt, 2004).

[7] While self-serving, Bremer's memoir amply demonstrates the "total failure of the Iraqi security forces." See L. Paul Bremer, *My Year in Iraq* (New York: Simon & Schuster, 2006), especially pp. 328–32. For the failure of those forces in Fallujah, see also Bing West, *No True Glory* (New York: Bantam, 2005) especially pp. 185–220.

[8] McCaffrey Report, 3.

[9] Quoted by Lt. Gen. David Petraeus, "Learning Counterinsurgency: Observations from Soldiering in Iraq," *Military Review* LXXXVI:1 (January–February 2006): 2–3. For an overview of the challenges of American adaptation to counter-insurgency warfare, see Max Boot, "The Struggle to Transform the Military," *Foreign Affairs*, March/April 2005, 103–18.

[10] Thomas M. Cooke, "NGA Support Teams Stand with the Warfighter," *Pathfinder*, Official NGA Publication, January 2006, 19.

[11] Greg Anderson, "'Reachback' Capability Makes a Difference in Iraq," *Pathfinder*, Official NGA Publication, January–February, 2006, 13–15.

[12] Cooke, op. cit., 18.

[13] McCaffrey Report, 4.

[14] "Pete" is a nom de guerre of this Army battalion commander who requested anonymity.

Epilogue

· · · · ·

t had been another long trip, not the mind-numbing, eyelid-drooping jet lag of a trip to the Middle East, but zigzagging across the country to give four speeches in three days—interrupted by network news hits—had taken a toll. The audiences had included corn farmers in Iowa as well as business executives in New York City. Never having been to Iowa, I was curious about its pivotal quadrennial role as the First Winnower of presidential candidacies and asked the Democrats in the room to please stand. When they shuffled smilingly to their feet, I suddenly shouted, "WHAT WERE YOU THINKING OF LAST TIME?" We shared a good-humored laugh, quickly followed by my reassurance that here was an equal-opportunity curmudgeon with disdain for both parties. "Next time, ask the Democratic candidates, 'If we withdraw from Iraq, where will we stand next, with whom and for what?' And ask the Republicans, 'Why was there no mobilization of this country after 9-11 and why has there been such uneven sacrifice ever since?'" That comment hit a nerve. A local Iowa boy, a reservist, had been killed in Iraq the week before, leaving a pregnant wife and a small child. The wound was fresh and throbbed painfully in the tight-knit rural community that instinctively reached out to neighbors. In contrast, the 9-11 attacks seemed distant memories, tragedies in even more distant cities rather than an assault on the nation.

The circuit next included one of those cities; the New York audience energized by the debate that had broken out when several retired generals had called for Donald Rumsfeld's resignation. Quickly labeled the "Revolt of the Generals," it was rare indeed for retired flag officers to indulge in public criticism of one of their political masters to whom they usually gave unstinting fealty—and in wartime, no less. Had they still been wearing the uniform, court-martials would have swiftly followed. But with Iraq continuing to fluctuate between political stalemate, insurgency, and civil war, the chickens were at last coming home to roost. The Army had been overruled, time and again being given short shrift by

Rumsfeld, but it had gamely saluted and gone on with the mission as best it could. Now it took the first steps toward ensuring the survival of the larger institution, and put a marker in place so that it might not be blamed for the mistakes of the politicians. As had been the case with Robert McNamara in 1968, an extended war was inevitably turning first upon its organizers. By now there was little doubt that the Army had been stretched well beyond any prudent limits. In Baghdad I had eaten dinner with a brigadier general who proudly noted that one of his best captains owed his superb performance at least in part to having survived six combat tours in eight years of commissioned service. "Of course," the brigadier noted in a quick afterthought, "he is no longer married but that couldn't be helped."

Other retired generals stoutly jumped to Rumsfeld's defense.[1] Three of the most prominent were the present and former Chairmen of the Joint Chiefs of Staff as well as the former CENTCOM commander, Gen. Tommy Franks, but all owed their retention or advancement in office to the defense secretary. Some suggested that breaking ranks was a violation of the American civil-military tradition, others that the debate would hurt the morale of the troops on duty in Iraq. Wes Clark joyfully jumped into the middle of the fray, arguing as strongly as ever that retired generals had a perfect right to voice their disagreements, many of which reflected his own earlier campaign positions and where had those guys been then, hey? Wes was the only one of the Warheads to call for the secretary's resignation, although Lou Dobbs tried mightily to entice Dave Grange into joining the Jacobin ranks, but was clearly no match for the general's adept footwork.

What was slightly disconcerting in the middle of the controversy was a conversation with one of the Warheads who had remained mysteriously quiet, despite his rather well-known sentiments. When I asked why he hadn't been heard from, he replied, "Well, Ken, you really *can* take these things too far." I was one of the world's greatest living authorities on taking things too far but had no clue what he meant. "Actually, I'm on the board of directors of three companies with defense contracting interests and it would be a breach of my fiduciary responsibilities to them if I were to take a public position in opposition to the Pentagon leadership." Actually many defense firms had such provisions in their employment contracts, but the potential conflict of interest appeared to be with the TV audience who had a presumptive right to his possibly wrongheaded, maybe misinformed but straight-from-the-shoulder position on the issues. I had never known one of the Warheads to offer an opinion on television that was in any way shaded by these other affiliations; but our ex parte attachments probably needed to be scrutinized as carefully as our credentials. Our media roles were truly modest and Rick Francona had undoubtedly been correct when he characterized us as "bit players, the hired help brought in to help handle the rush at Christmas."

But if there was an audience out there, they had a perfect right to expect our independent judgment.

The controversy was still going strong when the lecture tour concluded in Florida with two campus appearances arranged by another MSNBC colleague, terrorism analyst Walid Phares. It was pure fun because in addition to Walid, this gig meant being paired with two other Warheads, Bill Cowan of Fox and that unforgettable piece of work, Jack Jacobs. Just before we entered the auditorium, Jack quickly gathered us into a huddle for what I assumed was the latest skinny on Rumsfeld or network gossip.

"So a guy goes to the doctor with symptoms and the doctor runs all kinds of tests. The next week he comes back and the doctor says to him:

> Doc: "I've got bad news. You have two terrible diseases. The first is an STD that we are going to have to treat very aggressively with drugs and some very painful and intrusive procedures."
>
> Guy: "Oh my God! That's horrible! What could be worse? But you said I have *two* diseases—what's the other one?"
>
> Doc: "I'm afraid the other disease is Alzheimer's."
>
> Guy: "Well at least I don't have the clap!"

We laughed until the tears came, laughed so hard that we tried to shush each other and only made things worse, laughed so hard that it looked for a moment as if the start of the program might have to be delayed. Eventually we made it to the front of the auditorium, seated ourselves, and settled in for the panel. None of us dared look at Jack with his usual deadpan expression, now holding forth to an audience composed mostly of senior citizens enjoying their retirement.

A good number appeared to be aging veterans of World War II, who probably could have offered some risqué jokes of their own, but they found it difficult to understand why we were having such chronic problems raising the number of soldiers required for service in Iraq and elsewhere. Did we need to reinstate the draft? None of the Warheads believed that a return to the draft was a good idea because the professional force was far more proficient in adapting to the demands of counterinsurgency warfare. There were other alternatives such as shorter enlistments or even a "tiered" system of national service. The dean of American military sociologists, Professor Charles Moskos, had explored many of these options and even suggested linking some of them to a realignment of federal education benefits, famously observing that the present system produced "the GI Bill without the GI."[2]

The problem was that in 2004 we had held an election without ever examining these alternatives or even acknowledging that we might have a problem worthy of a national conversation. We had simply deluded ourselves, not challenging our leaders or questioning their assumptions. Instead we had implicitly embraced the idea of war on the cheap, betting on the forlorn hope that this conflict would be easy and soon ended, while recklessly assuming that victory would be won with "clean" high technology rather than dusty boots firmly astride the enemy's throat while controlling his territory. At best this was a naïve misreading of history, at worst a shameful disdain of its lessons. It was also the oldest of all military follies, a classic underestimation of the enemy, of his ability to endure, of his intent to prevail. Bill Cowan, himself a former Marine who had specialized in special operations in the Middle East and knew something of the enemy, chilled the audience with these words: "This may well be another Fifty or even a Hundred Years War. But if we do it right and get lucky, then it may turn out to be only Thirty."

His comment suggested an underlying truism—that armies do not go to war, but that nations do. And here was an even more fundamental problem, because evidence was growing that as a nation, America was either asleep or indifferent, collectively distanced by the shared nonexperience of Yossi's Gap. For the grandchildren of the Greatest Generation, military service was at best an irrelevant distraction. Former NBC anchor Tom Brokaw had briefly created a stir when he addressed the annual gathering of the Association of the United States Army in October 2005:

> Indisputably the United States has the finest military in the history of mankind.... Unfortunately it is also a military that in too many families, in too many communities and, especially, in too many corporate suites, board rooms, country clubs and other gathering places for the elite, it is a military that is out of sight and out of mind. It is separate and distinct from the day-to-day concerns of too many Americans, especially the elites with their hands on the levers of power. That is not just inappropriate; it is unacceptable and even dangerous to a democratic society.[3]

I had read Tom's words not long thereafter and was struck by how such trenchant comments had largely fallen on deaf ears. Shortly thereafter, he anchored a special that aired on NBC in prime time, movingly profiling the role of the reserves and the sacrifices being made in Iraq every day by those "other people's kids" from small town America. The special came and went yet life went, on as before. Had people forgotten just why we had a free press in the first place?

Apparently they had, or at least were not willing to turn down their IPods long enough to listen. By this point I was reading the galley proofs of a new book called *AWOL: The Unexcused Absence of America's Upper Classes from Military Service— And How It Hurts Our Country*.[4] It was enough to make you nuts. The authors, Kathy Roth-Douquet and Frank Schaeffer, had the goods, documenting the maddening outlines of "the disconnect" between the all-volunteer military and the larger society it was meant to serve. Yossi's Gap had now widened into a chasm between the classes. Roth-Douquet, a lawyer, Democratic activist, and (contrary to all prevailing expectations) Marine Corps wife, had a soccer mom's ear for social nuance, flawlessly capturing the unconscious snobbery of another mother: "I've raised my sons to be sensitive to others, and to be critical thinkers, so I don't think they'd be well suited for the military."[5]

Schaeffer's son had graduated from an elite New England prep school, announcing his enlistment in the Marine Corps from the podium. Instead of tears, cheers, and a standing ovation, Schaeffer overheard a fellow parent whisper, "I think we need to examine very carefully what went wrong here." But you could hardly blame the upwardly mobile for imitating—consciously or unconsciously—the behavior of the truly elite:

> Not too long ago the sons of presidents, bankers and oilmen regularly served. This was even true for members of the powerful dynasties such as the Roosevelts, the Kennedys, the Sulzbergers [owners and publishers of the *New York Times*] and the Bushes. Now, however, not one grandchild from those powerful dynasties serves. The last president with a child (or son-in-law) in uniform was Lyndon Johnson.[6]

Those same conspicuous absences were true of Hollywood actors or those few professional athletes not currently under investigation, indictment, or on trial. Some of my earliest memories of my dad were when he took me to Boston's Fenway Park, pointing out the tall right fielder as the immortal Ted Williams. One of the greatest hitters of all time, Williams's home run totals would have been even higher had he not served as a Marine Corps aviator in both World War II and Korea. Now some of the loudest voices celebrating the voluntary service of the late Arizona Cardinals star Pat Tillman—tragically killed in Afghanistan in 2004—came from those least likely to have considered service to country as a personal obligation.

The authors of *AWOL* had also included in their bill of particulars the poo-bahs of academe to whom we had entrusted the training of the next generation. As was so often the case with outsourcing, the hidden costs were killing us. The anti-Vietnam syndrome was still alive and well in academe's cloisters and tax-supported warrens. Stories abounded of students pressured by reflexively antiwar professors, of Reserve Officers' Training Corps (ROTC) detachments harassed by campus activists, even of campus access by military recruiters only grudgingly conceded by other self-appointed activists who considered them aliens unwelcome in the academic hive. In a way it was a form of institutional racism, not of course in the expression of hostility toward different racial or ethnic groupings but rather in the thought patterns: the same casual disdain for others, the same reference to unthinking stereotypes in accounting for differences, the same tired intellectual habits too long grown comfortable with unexamined assumptions.

Eliot Cohen had been one of the few highly credentialed academics with the courage to speak out against the prevailing cultural norms. In a widely noted editorial, Cohen had decried the overwhelming vote in 2005 by the faculty senate of Columbia University to ban ROTC from returning to their campus. He had used strong terms like "contemptible" and "churlish" to describe this latest missed opportunity to help reunite the military and academic institutions. But the words that surely must have resonated like a grenade in the faculty club were the ones he used to introduce the op-ed. The quotation he chose was a favorite of soldier-scholars and came from a nineteenth-century English historian: "The nation that will insist upon drawing a broad line of demarcation between the fighting man and the thinking man is liable to find its fighting done by fools and its thinking by cowards."[7] It was doubtful if Eliot had received many Seasons Greetings cards from Columbia later that year.

But our Florida seminar was now nearing its conclusions with a few last questions, some of them just variations of subjects covered earlier. "Gentlemen, why are all these retired generals calling for Secretary Rumsfeld's resignation at this late date? Why now?" Walid and Bill took some healthy cuts at that one and then it was my turn. Maybe it was late in the day, but this seemed like a hanging curve ball, the temptation was irresistible and I stepped into the swing. "Sir, I know some of those gentlemen, they went public for many different reasons, but the main one has to do with what you and the American public *did not do* during the election of 2004: to demand some straight answers to some hard questions." There was scattered applause as I passed the mike over to Jack even while the questioner persisted, "But shouldn't they have resigned instead—while they were still on active duty?" Jack smiled. At the war college, he had taught many of the officials now defending Rumsfeld, and I had earlier teased him by threatening to argue that the entire controversy was entirely his fault.

But now Jack rode to the rescue as he had done many times before, quietly saying that resignation was one of the few features that had not been imported into the American military culture from the British as so many others had. It was perfectly honorable in their system for an officer to resign if he found himself unable to agree with the basic policy or its implementation. Far from insubordination it was even considered a demonstration of the highest form of institutional loyalty. The American system had instead emphasized practicality: If I am commanding troops in the field, then my highest duty is training and taking care of them. Resignation might be morally satisfying but would effectively mean abandoning them. But perhaps now was the time to reexamine whether resignation might be the better option. Jack now revealed to the audience that as both a former instructor and as a friend, he had told Gen. Eric Shinseki, the former Army chief of staff, that it had not been enough merely to have testified before the Senate that 200,000 troops might eventually be needed in Iraq. When it became apparent that Shinseki was being overruled, Jack felt his highest moral duty was simply to resign. "I have always been influenced by the teachings of Rabbi Ben-Hillel, one of Judaism's most influential thinkers. And those teachings can be summed up by the questions: If not you, then who? And if not now, then when?"

At that moment, it would have been difficult to add much to what Jack—one of two living Medal of Honor recipients who were Jewish—had just said. We were good friends and colleagues, the back-and-forth teasing nearly constant. But whenever we were together I was always conscious, at some level, that the Medal of Honor he wore was meant to serve as a living example more than anything else. At some obscure battlefield half a world away and a generation earlier, Jack had answered Hillel's two questions in the only way that really mattered.[8] Against every reasonable expectation, he had lived to tell the tale. Now he had passed along those intensely personal questions as a challenge for the larger audience we so often address in television's virtual reality: If not you, then who? And if not now, then when? We were, of course, getting way above our Warheads pay grades, but these were precisely the right questions to leave with an American electorate that had failed to focus on the real issues during the last election. And now the clock was ticking louder than ever: Iraq teetering on the brink of civil war, Iran's ayatollahs sounding more like Nazis every time they opened their mouths, and America's underguarded borders overwhelmed by seemingly unstoppable waves of illegal immigrants. Other than that, Mrs. Lincoln, how has the play seemed to you so far?

I now lived close to one of those borders, San Antonio having become my newly adopted home town and a welcome refuge after enduring four Gulf Coast hurricanes in eighteen months. It was also the city of the Alamo—a parallel in American history to the heroic last stand of the 300 Spartans at Thermopylae over two thousand years ago—and as such, a fitting place to write this book. As I flew back to Texas, after bidding farewell to Jack and the others, it seemed doubtful if the implications of what we had said would ever catch on with the larger public. But an unexpected benefit of my work at the University of Texas at San Antonio had been the close contact with a unique group of visionaries who had produced some spectacular successes in transforming organizations—would that Donald Rumsfeld and the leaders of the American intelligence community had walked among them as well. One of these pioneers, Professor Robert Lengel, taught that "strategic conversations" are a fundamental first step for organizations in rediscovering "the commons"—the sense of who they are and what binds them together. Think Denzel Washington in *Remember the Titans*: same idea.[9]

Surely America is long overdue for a similar conversation and the election cycle beginning in 2006–2008 seems like an appropriate place to begin. We not only need to hear some straight talk about the threats that face us but also to summon up an answer to the same question Sean Connery asks so memorably in *The Untouchables*: "What are *you* prepared to do?" If we are tired of the Iraq war, it might be because we were content to fight it on the cheap and without truly engaging the great national engines of creativity, strength, and popular mobilization, which so animated and empowered the Greatest Generation. If we had the same concern about the impact the war on terror would have on our civil liberties, then maybe we would never have accepted responsibility for—or indeed even focused upon—the generations-long conflict that would be required to defeat the terrorists. And if we were worried about the widening gap between American society and those sent to defend it—well, actually, we weren't. All of which was one more reason to pencil ourselves in for a no-holds-barred strategic conversation—ideally one held in front of a full-length mirror.

I have always thought that it seemed futile to argue about a return to conscription before we were even sure we were asking the right questions. Because, in America, the questions that really matter are not those having to do with how many troops were needed, whether we should re-invent the format of national service, or even if educational benefits should be a reward for having fulfilled a universal obligation central to the nation's purpose. These questions are important but not the vital ones. Instead, the questions that really matter in strategic conversations are those in which the individual takes stock of who he or she is—and how that individual might answer the most fundamental questions of who we are as a people and what has become of us here of late.

Rabbi Hillel had given us two enormously helpful starting points—yet the inquiry was far older and inevitably involved the hidden recesses of the human spirit, regardless of one's definition of that term or even if one questioned the role that spiritual values might play in our national discourse. On the final leg of the journey home to San Antonio that night, my Bible fell open to a favorite Old Testament passage that was a personal turning point, and therefore an appropriate place to end this book:

> If my people, who are called by my name, shall humble themselves, and pray, and seek my face, and turn from their wicked ways; then will I see from heaven and will forgive their sin and will heal their land.[10]

---

[1] Touch-points of the controversy included articles by Maj. Gen. Paul Eaton, USA (Ret.), "A Top-Down Review for the Pentagon," *New York Times*, March 19, 2006; and Lt. Gen. Greg Newbold, USMC (Ret.), "Why Iraq Was a Mistake," *Time*, April 17, 2006, pp. 42–43. A contrary if largely unpersuasive view was offered by Lt. Gen. Michael DeLong, USMC (Ret.), "A General Misunderstanding," *New York Times*, April 16, 2006.

[2] See, for example, all by Charles Moskos, "Our Will to Fight Depends on Who Is Willing to Die," *Wall Street Journal*, March 20, 2002; "Feel that Draft?" *Chicago Tribune*, June 8, 2005; "A New Concept for the Citizen-Soldier," *Orbis*, Fall 2005, pp. 663–76; and "Saving the All-Volunteer Force," *Military Review*, May–June 2005, 6–7.

[3] Tom Brokaw, Speech to the Annual Convention, Association of the United States Army, Washington, DC, October 5, 2005.

[4] Kathy Roth-Douquet and Frank Schaeffer, *AWOL: The Unexcused Absence of America's Upper Classes from Military Service—And How It Hurts Our Country* (New York: Harper Collins, 2006).

[5] Ibid., 29.

[6] Ibid., 30.

[7] Sir William Francis Butler, quoted by Eliot A. Cohen "The Fighting Man and the Thinking Man," *Wall Street Journal*, May 13, 2005.

[8] According to Rabbi Joseph Telushkin, in *Jewish Literacy* (New York: William Morris & Company, 1991), 122, Hillel's full quote is: "If I am not for myself, who will be for me and, if only for myself, what am I? And if not now, when?"

[9] See Richard L. Daft and Robert Lengel, *Fusion Leadership* (San Francisco: Berrett-Koehler, 2000).

[10] The Holy Bible, II Chronicles 7:14, KJV.

Index

· · · · ·

About the Author

· · · · ·

Ken Allard is a former Army colonel who is forever being mistaken for someone of much greater distinction. The principal fault lies with the TV remote control, that cornerstone of the electronic era, which allows viewers to shift rapidly between various cable news channels on which the colonel and his Warhead colleagues interchangeably appear. For the record, MSNBC admits that "Colonel Ken" has been a principal military analyst for nine of its ten years on the air.

Such were the improbable results of one of the Vietnam War's last mistakes—when the Army drafted Ken Allard. They sent him first to Officer Candidate School and then to Germany, a country with which we were not, strictly speaking, at war just then. Educated far beyond his intelligence and in violation of any conceivable public purpose, Ken Allard holds a master's degree from Harvard and a doctorate from the Fletcher School of Law and Diplomacy. His service on the faculties of West Point and Georgetown, and as Dean of Students at the National War College is today strongly denied by all three institutions. He admittedly volunteered for service in Bosnia, which seemed like a big deal at the time. But Army officials gleefully note that the colonel, after his final tour on active duty there with the 1st Armored Division, has been long and deservedly retired.

Ken has adopted San Antonio, Texas, as his latest hometown, although there is some talk that local authorities may demand a recount.